PRIVATE

HONG KONG

东西汇合

PRIVATE
HONG KONG
完 *Where East Meets West* 完

BY SOPHIE BENGE

PHOTOGRAPHY BY FRITZ VON DER SCHULENBURG

ABBEVILLE PRESS PUBLISHERS

NEW YORK   LONDON   PARIS

Jacket Front: Lunch is set on the veranda of David Tang's house in Sai Kung Country Park.

Jacket Back: Top Row, left to right: see pages 97; 23; 182. Center Row, 186; 155; 57. Bottom Row, 62; 124; 176.

First published in the United States of America 1997
by Abbeville Press Inc.
488 Madison Avenue, New York, N.Y. 10022.

Created by Co & Bear Productions (UK) Ltd.
Copyright © 1997 Co & Bear Productions Ltd.
Photographs copyright © 1997 Fritz von der Schulenburg

Printed and bound in Italy.

First edition
10 9 8 7 6 5 4 3 2 1

PUBLISHING DIRECTOR   Beatrice Vincenzini
CREATIVE DIRECTOR   Charles Orchard
PROJECT MANAGER   David Shannon

Library of Congress Cataloging–in–Publication Data
Benge, Sophie.
   Private Hong Kong: where East meets West / by Sophie Benge ;
photography by Fritz von der Schulenburg.
            p.   cm.
   Includes index.
   ISBN 0-7892-0342-1
   1. Interior decoration—Hong Kong. 2. Decorative arts—China.
3. Furniture—China. I. von der Schulenburg, Fritz. II. Title.
NK2083.B46 1997
747.295125—dc21   97-21956

CONTENTS

PREFACE
by David Tang 8

WHERE EAST MEETS WEST

The True Meaning of Ming 12

Changing Spaces 18

Imperial Seat 24

Peak of Perfection 34

Italian Spirit 40

Block Magic 46

Tasteful Junk 52

Distinctive Tang 60

Terrace Treasure 68

Indian Rhapsody 74

Private View 80

A Beautiful Obsession 86

Cool Customers 94

Firm Favorite 102

Country Life 112

Style Counsel 118

Potted History 124

Quality Street 130

The Color of Money 138

Living by Design 146

Ace of Clubs 152

Aladdin's Cave 160

Model Elegance 166

House of Bullion 176

Jungle Hideaway 182

CHINESE INFLUENCE

Eastern Decorative Arts 192

RENDEZVOUS

Hong Kong Lifestyle 200

Visitor's Guide 210

INDEX

PREFACE

前言

CHINESE MEN WERE ASKED, in a recent survey in Hong Kong, why they got out of bed in the middle of the night. Ten percent said because they wanted a drink of water and another ten percent said because they wanted to go to the lavatory. Eighty percent said because they wanted to go home. Such, I suppose, is the importance of the home in Hong Kong and, if one would believe it, uxoriousness.

Little wonder then that wives in Hong Kong should wish to ensure the return of their husbands, Chinese or otherwise, even in the middle of the night, by beautifying their homes. And many beautiful examples are glimpsed in this colourful volume. The reader will find an eclectic collection of designs – some unashamedly Western, others fiercely traditional Chinese and others a kaleidoscope of East and West.

The juxtaposition of the Occident and the Orient is, I suppose, the most noticeable characteristic of a great many homes shown here. And what better place than Hong Kong in which to find them. It is first and foremost a Chinese city (95 percent of the inhabitants here are Chinese), yet a Martian might not think so from the air and mistake it for New York.

There are other oxymorons: in this city, there is a great deal of talk about face and feng shui, yet there is equally a great deal of talk about Adam Smith (usually unknowingly) and Rolls Royces. People chew ducks' feet and slurp up swallows' spit, but they also devour caviar and bite through T-bone steaks. Equally, they revel in the Chinese festivals of Ching Ming and Chung Yeung, but also enjoy the Queen's Birthday and Easter.

Hong Kong, therefore, sits comfortably on the horn of a great cosmopolitan crescent moon. Indeed, so comfortably that it verges on arrogance, and its successes have become the envy of the universe. Hong Kong has one of the world's lowest tax rates. It imports more Cognac Brandy than any other place, and is the world's second largest exporter of clothing. There are some surprises as well: Hong Kong has the world's highest per capita usership of public libraries; runs one of the most expensive tree-preservation schemes; and is among the world's leading breeding centres for endangered species. Eighty percent of Hong Kong's territory is rural; over half its population lives in subsidised housing; and most important of all perhaps, Hong Kong has the world's highest life expectancy rates.

So it is amongst these oscillating statistics that the people of Hong Kong live their lives, some of them in great comfort and style – comparable with anywhere in the world – as will be seen in the pages that follow. I have been to most of the homes in this book because I know most of the people behind them, and looking through the photographs I am reminded of how, when I first saw them, I scrutinised the interiors. It is a pity that not more bathrooms appear in this pristine volume because that small room often speaks a lot about the general taste of the resident. I never pass over a visit nor cease looking at everything in the bathroom before dinner: that is usually my proper start to the evening.

But of course it is through the sitting room and dining room that the homes really shine, although I always try to notice how my host and hostess *treat* their furniture. Do they worry about the carpet? Do they worry about the perspiring glasses or the steaming cups on their tables? Do they rush for bigger ashtrays or panic when they find none on seeing a huge cigar being lit, or a loquacious guest with a long stem of ash dangling perilously at the end of her cigarette? Another detail game one can play is to have a check list:–

1. Are there books in the room (a really bad sign if there aren't), and if so what are they? (Bad news if they are newly leather bound or hollow; better news if the creases show that they have been read, and best news if they contain some Woodhouse or Bryson or any poetry, especially Donne.)

2. Is the television boxed up? (Rather sissy, even if it is inside a piece of antique furniture; God forbid in a bespoke new one like in a hotel.)

3. What is the music? (Kenny G and Vivaldi's *Four Seasons* totally unacceptable; *Nessum Dorma* and Mozart's 21 a little cringing, whilst the Beatles and any *full* length opera would be acceptable – but best of all, no music.)

4. Is the host wearing a tie and the hostess wearing as much make-up as she would when going out? (If yes to both, then the dinner will *probably* be intolerable.)

5. Are women served before the men? (Very stupid practice as it prolongs the total time and allows heat to escape hot dishes – especially irritating with Chinese food - and unnecessarily bourgeois. The maxim of service ought to be: *citius quam asparagi conquunter*, quicker than asparagus is cooked!)

6. Are there clocks and are they antique and do they click and chime? (If yes then full marks.)

7. What are the paintings like? (Large lithographs by anyone are unacceptable; so are any badly framed pictures. In fact, the frame often gives away more about taste than the art! And how are they lit? Any picture lights that affix on the wall show a lack of detail – they should always be attached to the painting itself – and if they are angle-poised from the ceiling, then the chances are that the painting is not as good as it might be.)

Such behaviour of people in their homes is, to me, as important as their environment. But in a volume like this, the reader will not be able to appreciate what happens when these pretty pictures are put into use. Nonetheless, a glance through the homes here will at least offer some starting point and prepare the imagination for more. Not everyone will be as observant as, say, Henry James, whose acute sense of observation has always given me (and others naturally) a more acute sense of awareness of what to look for. In his *English Hours* for example, he wrote:

". . . . The place is inhabited, "kept up", full of the most interesting and most splendid detail . . . . Everything that in the material line can render life more noble and charming has been gathered into it with a profusion which makes the whole place a monument to past opportunity. As I wandered from one rich room to another and looked at these things that intimate appeal to the romantic sense which I just mentioned was mercilessly emphasised . . ."

Of course not many of us have the convoluted mind of Henry James, but it is always a treat to come across exteriors and interiors of homes that excite the senses – even though they can irritate us for not having thought of this or that ourselves. As the Bard once said:

"O, how bitter a thing it is to look into happiness through another man's eyes."

DAVID TANG   9

THE TRUE MEANING OF MING

明的真意

CHRISTIE'S AUCTION OF PIECES from the Museum of Classical Chinese Furniture in California, which was held in New York in the fall of 1996, grossed U.S. $11.2 million, the highest sum raised from any Chinese works of art sale in this decade. It represented to the world at large the phenomenal escalation of interest in Ming furniture, which began on a global scale only 15 years earlier, when the bamboo curtain was lifted and many forms of Chinese furniture were introduced to the outside world for the first time. Only in the spring of 1997 did New York's Metropolitan Museum of Art reinstall its Ming furniture in its Chinese galleries, while the first permanent gallery in China devoted to the furniture was opened as recently as 1996 at the Shanghai Museum of Art.

The interest and the subsequent expanding market for Ming furniture are due, to a significant extent, to Grace Wu Bruce, a leading dealer based in Hong Kong. She claims to have walked into the subject by accident but, struck by the sheer beauty of Ming, she became a "fiendish and passionate" collector until her knowledge, her contacts, and her hunger for the subject led her naturally into dealing.

OPPOSITE *In a fabric-lined corner of the drawing room hangs an oil by the modern Chinese artist Lin Fengmian, whose style was influenced by the work of the Impressionists after a visit she made to France in the 1920s.*

ABOVE *An exceptional Ming Dynasty chair with traditional soft matting seat and stiles to enhance stability. A scarcity of Ming chairs on the market in the mid-1990s prompted dealers to urge collectors no longer to wait to buy pairs.*

13

The tidal wave of excitement started in 1985 when *Classic Chinese Furniture*, the definitive book by the Beijing expert Wang Shixiang, was published. The restoration warehouse where Grace worked as a polisher quickly became a gallery and she herself soon earned a reputation among collectors as a leading connoisseur.

"The West discovered Chinese furniture before the Chinese did," says Marc Wilson, director of the Nelson-Atkins Museum in Kansas City. American and European diplomats and academics who collected and studied it while living in Peking from the 1930s to the 1950s took their collections with them when they were repatriated at the time of the Cultural Revolution. Until China opened up 30 years later, purchasing was relatively restricted in the West. Ming furniture does not seem to have been much appreciated by the Chinese populace, who ranked it below the greater arts of painting, calligraphy, and ceramics. The golden age of Chinese furniture began in 1567, when the decorative honey-colored huanghuali wood was first imported to China, and

OPPOSITE *A Ming daybed is now used as a coffee table. Stools such as these are the traditional form of seating except on more formal occasions. The scroll painting is by Harold Wong, whose works are collected by many American museums.*

TOP RIGHT *Like most 16th-century canopied beds, known as* jiazichuang, *this one has detachable posts and railings. Many Ming-period prints feature the canopied bed, whose drapes were drawn at night to create a room within a room.*

BOTTOM RIGHT *An 18th-century ship's desk-chest of hong mu wood stands in a corner of the guest bedroom, with an 18th-century stool at the foot of the bed.*

closed with the fall of the last Ming emperor, who hanged himself outside the walls of the Forbidden City in 1644.

It has been said that "Western cabinetmakers are blacksmiths, while the Chinese are jewellers." As one would expect, Grace's home is a crown set with some of the best jewels: exceptional examples of classic designs for chairs, tables, cabinets, and stools, their rich patinas beautifully matched by the equally rich color scheme on walls and soft furnishings.

The 16th- and 17th-century furniture, made entirely from tropical hardwood down to the very dowels and pins, is complemented by accessories and objects from the same period and the best of classical Chinese calligraphy and brush painting. Through her years of experience and her contacts among the Ming cognoscenti, Grace is aware of all furniture that comes on the market. Some of the finest specimens now grace her home. As she observes, "It is the purity of the design, architectural proportions, and exquisite craftsmanship that appeals to Western and Eastern collectors alike. No other culture has produced furniture as beautiful in its integration of design and structure." 完

OPPOSITE *The drawing room boasts a pair of rare Ming Dynasty chairs. On top of the Ming clothes chest is an 18th-century, Yongzheng period brush pot and a sculpture crafted from tree roots.*

ABOVE *In China calligraphy is considered the highest form of art. These two scrolls are by Lin Sanzhi. The painting behind the table is by Zhang Daqian. The group of monochrome ceramics are from the Kangxi period of the 17th century, while the table is a rare example of what is known as the "four sides flushed" construction with a solid plank top, a much-coveted feature.*

TOP RIGHT *The sloping-style cabinet is one of the most ingenious designs in Ming furniture. The main stiles, recessed from the top corners, slope out in a subtle splay and hold the doors, making hinges unnecessary.*

RIGHT *Grace's private gallery of Chinese art includes works by Wu Guanzhong, Lin Sanzhi, and a portrait of Grace by Chiu Ya Tsai.*

CHANGING SPACES

变化多端

KAMWA AND MICHELLE CHAN are pioneers in Hong Kong of a personalized approach to living. Their philosophy that good taste need not be sacrificed at the altar of high design first came to public attention in 1995 when they opened Iglu, Hong Kong's first one-stop lifestyle shop. Their apartment above is a continuation of the shop below, filled with furniture designed to be comfortable and practical. "People think that if they buy Gucci they are in good hands. That is not what we are about," says Kamwa, who runs the couple's trendsetting shop and specializes in packaging and interior concepts for new companies.

The Chinese-Cambodian couple returned to Hong Kong after 33 years of living in five European countries and in America, working in the fields of fashion and graphic design. They are members of a new cosmopolitan breed of Southeast Asians who have returned from life in the West with an intellectual vision of good living that is very different from mainstream Chinese thought. As the world has grown increasingly homogenized, high-tech, and hard-edged, they have taken refuge in a softer, more individual focus at home. "We do our own thinking,"

OPPOSITE *Downstairs in Iglu, the lifestyle shop the couple opened in 1995. They are the sole Hong Kong agents for Bulthaup kitchens.*

ABOVE *This table is an old piece by Italian designer Ettore Sotsass. Michelle's silver betelnut boxes are from Cambodia.*

LEFT *This view from the roof terrace is typical in downtown Hong Kong. It was one reason for renting the property, as both Kamwa and Michelle remember playing on roofs as children—he in Hong Kong for lack of an alternative and she in Cambodia, where it was not safe to play in the street.*

OPPOSITE *The bedside drawing by Kamwa announced the birth of the couple's daughter, Jeanne. An old Shaker quilt covers the bed, while the mosquito net is placed strategically above Kamwa's side because, he laments, his blood is sweet all year round.*

asserts Michelle. "We try to encourage people to see things in a new light and do things their own way."

A 1930s flat in the Wanchai district, their home felt cramped and gloomy when they moved in, but skillful refurbishment has transformed it. Designed for relaxation, it is now an easy configuration of open spaces, where the only closed door leads to the bathroom. The couple's bedroom is shielded from the living area by a set of suspended shelves designed by Kamwa to maintain the light, fluid feeling that pervades the apartment. The other end of the long,

rectangular room is raised and covered with tatami matting to add an extra dimension. This layout provides valuable storage space and can also be turned into a sleeping area for guests, who roll out futons at night. With only 1,000 square feet to play with, Kamwa and Michelle have learned to be imaginative and highly resourceful in their use of space.

While the couple hold that home should be a tranquil and restful place to recharge in, their flat-above-the-shop is nevertheless a shrine to their many years spent traveling and working overseas. It is packed to the gunwales with pieces bought in America, Germany, France, Holland, and Italy. Much of the furniture comes from Italy, as they lived in Milan for many years. Among their most exciting acquisitions are a pair of 1950s Prada display cabinets that they discovered on a rubbish heap in Milan. Other collectors' items include a standing lamp by Philippe Starck and rare Beatles photographs.

All in all the apartment reflects the gradual shift in opinion in Hong Kong, whereby cooking is no longer solely the maid's domain, pottery is valued above porcelain, and a coffee grinder is considered a better investment than a crocodile handbag. 完

OPPOSITE *Christian Liaigre furniture on display in Iglu. The French designer's theory that decorative elements distract from the natural beauty of integrated forms fits perfectly with the couple's philosophy that good design is synonymous with easy, practical living.*

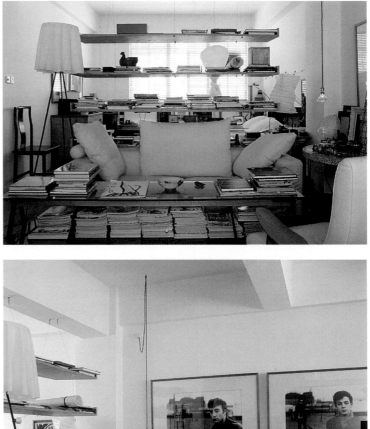

ABOVE *This original Fortuny lamp resembles the flashgun that was used in early professional photography.*

TOP RIGHT *Magazines from many countries have been collected and kept as a source of inspiration. For many years Kamwa contributed drawings for publication in German* Vogue.

RIGHT *Rare collectors' items, the photographs of John Lennon and Paul McCartney were taken by Astrid Kirchher, girlfriend of original Beatle Paul Sutcliffe. Kamwa bought them from her in Hamburg, where they were taken during the Beatles' first visit to the city in the early 1960s. The Kilim rug was bought in Amsterdam.*

IMPERIAL SEAT

皇座

IT IS NOT A BUILDING of any great architectural merit, but it remains the largest residence in Hong Kong and, in its more recent history, was the base for the Byzantine negotiations that set the territory on course for an event unique in history: the peaceful transfer of sovereignty over a major city at a date decided more than a decade in advance. On the arrival of Britain's twenty-eighth and last governor of Hong Kong, Chris Patten, Government House still clung to its colonial air. It was high time that the official heart of Britain's presence here should reflect the creative genius of Hong Kong's East-meets-West personality. To this end a thorough refurbishment (costing HK $10 million) took place in 1993.

"Chris and I hoped to make it less a symbol of British colonialism and more a house that belonged to the Hong Kong people," says Lavender Patten, the governor's wife. The black-and-white marble hallway, dominated by paintings of former kings and queens of England, was replaced with a lighter decorative scheme that provided a harmonious backdrop for works by Hong Kong designers. Under the direction of the renowned Shanghainese architect Tao Ho and Hong Kong's Trade Development Council,

OPPOSITE AND ABOVE *Now in the heart of the city, in 1852 Government House was deemed by the* China Mail *to be "far too distant from the center of town for forenoon calls." By the 1980s the house was said by Chi Park Lai, the renowned geomancer, to be intimidated by its tall commercial neighbors; trees were planted on feng shui principles to deflect negative chi from the skyscrapers' sharp corners.*

25

TOP RIGHT *Colonial living. The governor's private area, where the Pattens would often take their breakfast, leads to a covered terrace ideal for alfresco dining.*

BOTTOM RIGHT *The pagoda—thought to represent a mouse, according to feng shui—was added in the 1980s as a distraction for the main house, the "cat."*

OPPOSITE *Norman Foster's Hong Kong and Shanghai Bank and I.M. Pei's Bank of China. Two willows and a bottlebrush tree were planted to the right of the fountain to prevent the house from being cut like a dagger by the sharp corners of the Bank of China that point directly toward the property.*

Government House was transformed into a showcase for local artisans and artists—makers of furniture, carpets, pottery, woodwork, and painting—while preserving its British heritage. English antiques now consort with glazed celadon pots, Taiwanese wooden sculptures, and numerous treasures on loan from the Hong Kong Museum of Art.

The house is a strange conglomeration of styles, several additions having been made over the years. The most unusual is that of a young Japanese architect who was commissioned to redesign the residence when the Japanese occupied Hong Kong during World War II. The main building was adapted during this period and an Asian-influenced, tile-roofed tower added for observation purposes.

However, by Christmas 1946 the then governor, Sir Mark Young, had jettisoned the Japanese tatami mats and Shoji screens that had been introduced into the upstairs rooms. The samurai warrior statues and the stuffed tiger, shot on the Stanley Peninsula in 1942, had been ejected from the hall and old rose cretonne from England was on order. Sadly, much of the former furniture, as well as pieces from a fine art collection left to the government by businessman

OPPOSITE *The carpet in the main hallway is one of four specially commissioned from a local manufacturer, Tai Ping. Its design celebrates the bauhinia, Hong Kong's official flower.*

ABOVE *This stairwell leads to the tower, added during World War II by the Japanese, partly as a way of linking the house to the ballroom, which was built at the turn of the century and left untouched by the Japanese. Then ruling lieutenant governor Rensuke Isogai never lived at Government House, preferring his accommodation at Repulse Bay on the south side of the island.*

Sir Paul Chater, were never rediscovered. But a bottle of brandy that a pre-war custodian of the house—with admirable forethought—had buried under a tree was successfully dug up. It apparently proved much the better for its four years laid to rest!

Until the arrival of the Pattens, post-war governors' wives had been given only small amounts of money with which to redecorate rooms as required. The decor had thus developed in piecemeal fashion in accordance with the tastes of five different women, and did not mirror the tremendous changes that have taken place in Hong Kong in the past 50 years. Now, appropriately, Government House bears testimony to the wealth of artistic talent that is constantly springing from Hong Kong's vibrant culture.

And it is not just royal visitors and foreign dignitaries who have benefitted from its resplendent new look. By hosting numerous parties, concerts, and charity functions the Pattens ensured that more visitors than ever before in the house's 140-year history have been invited to admire the riches of the interior and marvel at the rhododendrons for which the gardens are renowned. 完

OPPOSITE *The peach-and-cream color scheme of the drawing room was chosen, on advice from the geomancer, to suit the constitution of the last governor, Christopher Patten. Although all the fabrics came from England, they were used to recover existing furniture, for economy. English antiques have been mixed with Chinese elmwood furniture, as part of the East-meets-West theme for the 1990s renovation.*

LEFT *The ballroom's first royal guest was the British Prince of Wales, later King Edward VIII, in 1922. It was not fitted with air-conditioning until 1972, at which point the ceiling fans were replaced with these breathtaking chandeliers brought by a former governor's wife from a palace in India. The ballroom was used once a week during the Pattens' residency for charity functions and concerts.*

ABOVE *Photographs in the drawing room include several given to the Pattens by members of the British royal family when they visited; one is signed by Diana, Princess of Wales.*

ABOVE *Surrounded by lawns and lush planting, the swimming pool can be glimpsed from the governor's private office.*

OPPOSITE *The large, airy dining room at Government House is presided over by a portrait of Queen Elizabeth II.*

PEAK OF PERFECTION

绝对完美

ALISON HENRY IS A STANDARD-BEARER for Hong Kong's reputation as a land of opportunity. Her meteoric rise to the top of her profession was complete by the time she was 30, barely five years after arriving in the territory from London in 1990. She went from heading up the Hong Kong office of a British interior design firm to managing her own 18-strong company, Alison Henry Design. Her distinctive decorative style has changed the face of leading hotels (The Peninsula, Mandarin Oriental, and Excelsior) in the same way that it has shaped her own homes in Sydney, London, Thailand, and at one of the most prestigious addresses on The Peak, Hong Kong.

Her home is a high-caliber example of the East-meets-West style that is a trademark of the successful breed of expatriates who have made their home here and traveled extensively around the region, collecting as they go. Thailand, an especially popular source of decorative arts and antiques for Asian home building, has been a frequent port of call for Alison and her property-magnate husband, David Davies. Their impressive collection of opium pipes, silver boxes, lacquerware, and 32 Siamese Buddhas, together with pieces of Chinese furniture, are mixed

OPPOSITE *The ivory and black tones of the lounge room provide the backdrop for the couple's collection of antique Buddhas and Chinese silver hand-warmers, seen here displayed on trunks.*

ABOVE *The sofas were designed by Alison. The opium pipes and Cambodian silver boxes on the black lacquered bamboo trunks are some of the couple's many Asian artifacts.*

35

TOP LEFT *The clean black-and-white theme is continued in the couple's bedroom—and even influences their choice of clothes.*

BOTTOM LEFT *All four bathrooms in the apartment are graphic studies in white with black marble accents.*

OPPOSITE *The 10-seater dining table is overlooked by an abstract painting by the Chinese-Irish artist Gerard Henderson, who lives and works in Hong Kong.*

boldly with Alison's Western designs for soft furnishings. The professional in her has purposely kept the structural background of her apartment simple as a foil for her exuberant collection.

Not only is the whole apartment superbly coiffed, it shows an expert sense of layout and an overall mantle of style without any discordant notes—in other words, a harmonious whole of mix, match, tone, and tie-in.

In keeping with her belief that all features of an apartment should be determined by the layout, she completely overhauled the space, creating a central axis that drops down from a hip-height balustrade and sweeping steps to a large living and dining area on one side and cosier recesses on the other, making one fluid space. The focal point is a wall-to-wall window offering a stunning harbor view, punctuated in the center by a dramatic opium bed. "If modern places are without important pieces or antiques of scale it can look a bit wishy-washy," says Alison. She defines her taste as "strong and dramatic"—you won't find any spriggy prints in a Henry home. All is strictly color-coded to black and white because of the drama they create together. 完

OPPOSITE *Alison overhauled her 3,500 square foot space by creating a central axis that drops down to the living area. The design of the whole apartment makes it a stunning showcase of dramatic contrasts and Asian glamour. The scale of the gilded, inlaid mirror in the study area indicates that it was originally an important piece from a temple in Thailand.*

LEFT *The apartment commands some of the best views looking east along the north side of the island and across the harbor to Kowloon. Like many of the pieces here, this stately opium bed was bought in Thailand.*

ABOVE *A limited-edition humidor by David Linley, bought by Alison for her husband, on the Hong Kong leg of the 1995 exhibition world tour of David Linley's architectural humidors for Alfred Dunhill.*

ITALIAN SPIRIT

意大利式精神

THE APARTMENT OF ELISABETTA and Galeazzo Scarampi del Cairo di Pruney resembles a Piedmontese castello more closely than would seem possible on the ninth floor of a 1950s block in Hong Kong. A synthesis of Italian regional antiques, rich fabrics, family oils, and heirlooms, it is a perfect reflection of their aristocratic lineage.

Because of the demands of Galeazzo's career as an international private banker, it has been many years since the couple have lived in the countryside around Turin where they met. Yet despite the years based in New York and Hong Kong, the Italian spirit in the Scarampi family has not been diluted. That exuberant delight in *la dolce vita* is seen in the colorful quality of the decoration—Elisabetta makes a weekly pilgrimage to Kowloon's flower market to ensure that her home is never bare of blooms, and she buys cuts of meat from Hong Kong's most famous Italian restaurant so that she can cook authentic provincial dishes. Even the candies in the silver dishes are made in Italy to a special recipe.

"I came from a rich ambience of flowers, antiques, and paintings and my eyes got used to beautiful things," says Elisabetta in explanation of

OPPOSITE *A 19th-century blue-and-white vase—with the typical dragon, bat, and cloud motif —makes a striking centerpiece.*

ABOVE *The balcony, verdant with well-tended plants, is wide enough for a table surrounded by local rattan chairs—ideal for lazy lunches.*

41

OPPOSITE *A strong culture surrounds the Chinese tradition of tea drinking, valued for its thirst-quenching and purifying benefits. For centuries teapots have been intricately decorated as expressions of creative virtuosity.*

RIGHT *A detail of the bar. Amid the bottles and rows of sparkling glasses is a glorious bouquet created with some of the flowers that Elisabetta brings home from her weekly trips to Kowloon market.*

her taste for high European style. She worked as a professional interior designer in Piedmont before moving abroad, ultimately to Hong Kong. Here she has employed her well-honed eye to transform an ordinary middle-aged apartment into a venerable residence, with years of history and culture on display in every corner. Her sense of style includes mixing the old with the new, such as family silver with new silver boxes from Cambodia, and antiques with modern pieces of Italian lacquered furniture. Wall-to-wall carpets have been replaced by antique rugs, which, like the wallpaper borders bought specially in New York ("the best place for borders"), add to the time-honored and lived-in feeling that the home exudes.

The Scarampis are prominent members of the small Hong Kong community of 2,500 Italians, regular guests of the Italian Consul General and active members in the Dante Alighieri Italian cultural association. Their daughter, Lucrezia, attends school on Saturdays in order to study Italian, and the family returns home twice a year.

Elisabetta's natural talent for decoration and instinctive appreciation of quality have now drawn her into collecting fine Chinese arts and crafts. "My first passion is pottery," she confides. With the time and means to travel around the region extensively on buying trips, Elisabetta has become an expert through seeing and handling hundreds of pieces, and has acquired exquisite examples for her home. In Hong Kong she is in regular contact with trusted sources who keep her informed about the market. She talks eloquently about the history of her pieces but—like many a serious collector—she will fall silent when asked to reveal the names of her dealers. Those names are not for dropping. 完

43

OPPOSITE *Silver-framed photographs and a map of medieval Turin, the city from which the family originates, are strong reminders of the Scarampis' Italian heritage.*

ABOVE *Red lacquer furniture from Macau and a series of allegorical prints bought in Rome meet in the spare bedroom.*

RIGHT *Family heirlooms: an 18th-century Piedmontese walnut commode and a Louis XVI chair reflect the apartment's eclectic style.*

BLOCK MAGIC

神奇大厦

VIRTUALLY EVERY ITEM in this debonair apartment is of vintage design, collected over time by its architect owner. His conversation, peppered with intellectual observations on the interrelationships between art and society through the ages, convinces listeners that his home must be the embodiment of cerebral style. "If you have a great deal of decadence you can demand refinement," he declares, reflecting on the evolution of design in the 1980s and the prosperity of Hong Kong today. It could also be said of his own home, with its mantle of minimalist sophistication.

A Chinese bachelor educated at Harvard, he is a rarity among apartment dwellers in having a home of tailormade proportions: he is the architect of the block in which he lives. He designed all the flats with a long, narrow layout so that most rooms overlook the cinematic view down the tiers of skyscrapers leading to the harbor. Consequently, the main living space is just one attenuated room divided into three sections by the strategic positioning of large sofas. The decorative scheme takes its cue from the modernist movement, with signature pieces by Eileen Gray, Le Corbusier, and Gerrit Rietveld. But by far the most prominent features are the larger-than-life,

OPPOSITE *It is only in recent years that the vogue for entertaining at home has really taken off in Hong Kong; the owner of this apartment is one of the city's most celebrated hosts.*

ABOVE *This chandelier is a specially commissioned original by the Czech craftsman Boris Sipek. It arrived in pieces and had to be painstakingly assembled on site.*

47

TOP RIGHT *An original Biedermeier bookcase and a Memphis Group pedestal.*

BOTTOM RIGHT *This Philippe Starck side table in ebonized wood and steel metamorphoses into a chair when its top is lifted up. The rug, colored in natural dyes, is a reproduction from the estate of Eileen Gray.*

OPPOSITE *Opposites attract: giant "robotic" speakers contrast with the intricate artistry of an Art Deco nest of tables from Shanghai, made of stripped and refinished Chinese black wood. An original Biedermeier piece at the far end of the room faces a leather Le Corbusier sofa at the near end.*

two-tier Goldman speakers, suspended like robots on their hinges. "Once you have large speakers, you can never go back to smaller ones," proclaims this music fanatic who fell in love with them because they pander to both his passions: as well as supplying sensational sound they also make a definite design statement.

The apartment's overall color scheme is monochrome, with visual interest provided principally by the shape and contour of the contents, carefully chosen to reflect the owner's respect for quality craftsmanship and design. Splashes of color, such as an orange chiffon curtain and jewel-bright cushions, add a touch of zest to the carefully laid out interior. No clutter is ever permitted to disrupt the sense of immaculate completeness.

One of the three bedrooms has become a shrine to the owner's hobbies. His desk is covered with gilded trophies from the Classic Car Club, large ashtrays, and humidors. For when he is not designing apartment blocks in Hong Kong, this intellectual aesthete likes nothing better than to indulge in the very finest wines and cigars and be chauffeur-driven in his 1940s petrol blue Rolls-Royce. 完

TOP RIGHT *A Le Corbusier chaise longue is positioned vertiginously close to the window for enjoying the cinematic views of Mid Levels below.*

BOTTOM RIGHT *A propaganda painting above the spare bed was commissioned by an American printing company to commemorate the symbols of progress: industry, shipping, air travel, and high-rise construction.*

BELOW *This Rietveld chair sits below two prints, one of which depicts the same chair in its composition.*

OPPOSITE *An eclectic corner of the apartment displaying a range of styles and periods, including a modern reproduction of a Renaissance triptych, a Charles Rennie Mackintosh chair, and a 1940s chair bought at a London auction. The Chinese elmwood table is probably a turn-of-the-century commission piece, intricately carved with auspicious emblems such as pumpkins, peaches, and wild animals.*

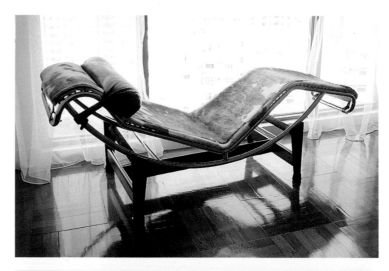

TASTEFUL JUNK

别树一格的帆船

HONG KONG HARBOR not only has one of the greatest concentrations of merchant shipping in the world, it also is home to countless leisure craft of every size and shape. You might imagine that no one vessel could stand out in this maritime multitude, but Kambiz Tabar's is one of a kind—truly a jewel of a junk.

Instantly recognizable by its distinctive stern (rounded rather than square as in traditional junks), it has a level of luxury that puts it in a wholly different league. No comfort has been forgone for the sake of living afloat. Bathrooms boast Italian marble basins, telephones on every side table can call any point on the globe, toilets flush electronically, and the Jacuzzi can easily accommodate eight.

Kambiz, a Persian marble dealer, designed the boat himself and then commissioned a shipyard—Sun Hing Shing on the island of Ap Lei Chan—to translate his designs into reality. Measuring 93 by 26 feet, it was built with two types of wood, teak and Indonesian yacol. Extremely hard—the stainless steel of woods—yacol was used for the keel, hull, ribs, ceiling beams, and most of the boat's infrastructure, while all other features were done in teak. Only

OPPOSITE *Mouthwatering meals taken on the middle deck are enhanced by soft sea breezes and glorious 180-degree views aft.*

LEFT *A marble dealer and connoisseur, Kambiz named his floating home after Michelangelo, the greatest of all sculptors in marble.*

perfection would do for Kambiz and the shipyard's master carpenters: the staircase leading below deck was rebuilt five times until it was judged to be right. The two 700 hp Rolls-Royce engines enable speeds of up to 18 knots, but rarely are they required to perform at such a pace. Intended to help Kambiz and his friends to unwind, the junk is geared toward a languorous lifestyle.

Beds, sofas, banquettes, and armchairs are unfailingly soft and inviting, while on the top deck recliners and a huge hammock seduce guests into

53

OPPOSITE *One of the well-appointed guest cabins, with bedlinens from Ralph Lauren. The brass porthole is one of 28 that were specially cast in France to an original design.*

TOP RIGHT *Drawing on his specialist knowledge of marble, Kambiz chose the most prized blue stone from Italy for the vanity units.*

BOTTOM RIGHT *The master cabin has the space and splendor of an ocean liner suite. The junk sleeps 13 in all (including the full-time crew of captain, his wife, and boatboy).*

sun-blessed slumbers. The fabrics throughout—selected by Alison Henry Design—are natural cottons and linens in relaxing neutral shades or refreshing patterns to complement the outdoor, holiday atmosphere.

Long, lazy lunches al fresco are savored under the covered deck, while in the evening everyone gathers in the paneled living room renowned for its Renoir painting. An unfinished oil of Renoir's maid Gabrielle, this fascinating portrait was done when she was 15; when Kambiz heard that she was still alive he visited her in the south of France and she shared with him her memories of sitting for Renoir. "Even the name of the painter makes you feel vibrant in your heart," says Kambiz. But it was Gabrielle's beauty that compelled him to buy the painting. Her face "is just a dream. She looks very shy."

It comes as no surprise to learn that Prince Albert of Monaco, Michael Caine, and Jeremy Irons have all enjoyed Kambiz's nautical hospitality. Even those accustomed to the very best of everything would leap at the chance of a weekend in the company of Kambiz, his affectionate labrador Mario, and his rare Renoir. 完

LEFT *The canopy on the top deck, unusual for a junk, provides shade for guests.*

BELOW *After dinner around the 10-seater table, guests can wander into the living room to enjoy a post-prandial sambuca and a private view of the Renoir.*

OPPOSITE *The galley is equipped with a full-size fridge and freezer, double sinks, a stainless-steel Parma ham slicer, and a well-stocked wine rack. Kambiz delights in rustling up gourmet dishes for his guests' delectation.*

DISTINCTIVE TANG

出色的邓家

"IT WAS THE HAPPIEST DAY of my life," says David Tang of the day he bought his beloved house in Sai Kung. He had been pestering the owner on a daily basis for about two years before. "I beat him up and tortured him," he jokes. But he finally won what he had been searching for: a house with a garden running down to the sea, of which there are precious few in Hong Kong. Because of his globetrotting lifestyle, it was also important to David that the house, in Sai Kung Country Park, was easily accessible by road, boat, and helicopter. He first spotted the house, in fact, when he flew over it in his helicopter.

Because David's country retreat lies in one of Hong Kong's environmentally protected areas, he was subject to "18 million regulations"; it took 24 months to get permission to build a tiny swimming pool compared with only 24 days to construct it. When he arrived not a single flower blossomed in the garden. He completely relandscaped the plot with a profusion of bougainvillea, azaleas, hibiscus, imported coconut trees, and more. He flattened the lawn, providing a perfect platform for a marquee that is hoisted often to entertain the stream of celebrities who party chez Tang when in town. Kevin Costner,

OPPOSITE *Guests often arrive at David's house by boat at the jetty beyond these mangrove swamps. A bronze sculpture of a boy perches above the water.*

ABOVE *A view of the house and landscaped garden over an expanse of lawn. Original 1970s smoked-glass windows were ripped out in favor of French doors.*

OPPOSITE *The small swimming pool that required two years of negotiations with the council before it could be built. The surrounding palm trees were brought in for a tropical flavor and the cannon came from Havana.*

RIGHT *The roof terrace of David Tang's house in Sai Kung Country Park is possibly the nearest thing to heaven in Hong Kong: not a sound disturbs the silence and there is no other building in sight.*

Michael Caine, and the Duchess of York are just some of the guests who can be seen enjoying Tang hospitality in the legions of photographs displayed throughout the house.

The building stands squarely facing the sea, a warm, light-filled place with a Mediterranean-style openness and French doors running the length of every floor. David has retained the one-room-per-floor format and decorated it in line with his sense of ordered chaos.

His exceptional taste has found favor with style aficionados everywhere, following his impresario ventures into chic clubs (China Club in Hong Kong and Beijing) and chic shops (Shanghai Tang in Hong Kong and soon New York), which have gained worldwide reputations for turning Chinese style into an international trend. At home his Anglophile side takes over. Out of a horror of minimalism he achieves his ordered chaos with bright colors, for cheerfulness; lots of paintings, artfully framed; a wealth of books (he reads four at the same time); Tang memorabilia (he's a shopaholic); and piles of humidors (he is always wreathed in a cloud of cigar smoke). Everything has been put together with what he calls "reckless prudence," which is his way of saying that he buys what he likes without knowing where he will put it. "This is the wonderful thing about not being a designer: you don't have to lay out a plan and be contrived."

Perhaps this philosophy contributes to the overriding sense of comfort here; this is a place where guests feel genuinely at home. It invites you to kick off your shoes and sink into one of the oversize sofas, designed to David's specifications—at least 34 inches deep and stacked high with cushions. 完

BELOW *Books are a prominent feature of David's house. An avid reader, he has built shelves in every available corner to hold his rapidly expanding collection. The decorative colored-glass mirror is by a London artist.*

RIGHT *The bathroom is fitted with Czech & Speake luxuries and a leather armchair. The painting is by Liu Wei, one of only two contemporary Chinese painters to exhibit in the Italian pavilion at the 1996 Venice Biennale.*

OPPOSITE *David's bed has been moved around on the advice of his feng shui master, who told him to change its position or it would lead to divorce. David changed it but still divorced, so he moved it back to this, his favored spot.*

BELOW *Racing green walls in the first-floor sitting room were chosen in contrast to those in the airy, white room shown opposite. "I like bold colors because I like to be cheerful most of the time," says David.*

RIGHT *An idiosyncratic Gothic–Revival gilt mirror hangs over this old painted dressing table bought from London. The table illustrates David's penchant for distressed furniture.*

OPPOSITE *When he stays at Sai Kung, David plays the piano before bed and on waking. Serendipity led him to buy this Steinway; he spotted it in a shop window in London while waiting for his girlfriend to buy bananas in the grocery store next door.*

TERRACE TREASURE

梯级藏宝

MIDWAY EN ROUTE to the seamless stretch of residential Mid Levels, there's a chink in the phalanx of tower blocks that stand sentinel over the central business district. A multistory car park brushes one ear, and 50 stories of flats the other, of what is the last remaining terrace in Hong Kong. The other 18 houses in the original strip have long since fallen prey to the bulldozer, but two survivors stand fast out of family respect for the late grandfather who was the owner-occupier from the terrace's construction in the 1930s until his death.

Given the general trend of Hong Kong development, there is precious little time left before this rare pocket of history is torn out to make way for a bigger and supposedly better building. In view of this, Yan and Sandra d'Auriol and their young family count their blessings. As long-time tenants they know how lucky they are to be enjoying the luxury of living under 21-foot-high ceilings and behind glass-and-teak paneled doors when so many people in Hong Kong are cocooned in a white washed shell on the forty-sixth floor of an apartment block.

The French-English couple have let the colonial profile of the house dictate its decorative style,

OPPOSITE *The d'Auriol family home is a rare sight in fin-de-siècle Hong Kong. Four stories tall and crowned by a roof terrace, it is a prime example of 1930s architecture.*

ABOVE *On top of an early 18th-century scholar's table stands a collection of Han Dynasty terra-cotta figures, original icons from the tombs of Chinese village elders.*

69

RIGHT *A Tang Dynasty horse stands in front of an 18th-century calligraphic rendering of the "tiger" character, which would have been executed as an artist's examination piece.*

OPPOSITE *The breakfast room at the front of the house would originally have been an open-sided terrace. The blue-and-white tile and terra-cotta floor was made in the nearby Portuguese colony of Macau.*

adding Chinese antiques and Asian art objects collected over years of traveling around the region. As passionate purchasers (the first port of call on a London business trip is Bermondsey market), they confess, "We always buy, but not always well. We want to create an environment with a Chinese atmosphere." After living here for nearly 17 years, Yan and Sandra have acquired some beautiful antique furniture no longer seen for sale, such as their enormous elmwood bed and wardrobe with rich patinas. However, after all this time in Hong Kong the couple's tastes are now veering away from what Sandra calls "the dowry chests with moon locks, the banana-shaped coffee table and ancestor portraits on the wall," because as part of every foreigner's A–Z portfolio of Chinese antiques these pieces are no longer so original.

Their favorite room in the house is the bathroom, converted from the original veranda at the front into a luxurious den of cream and marble. Sandra spends a lot of her time there because it is the brightest room. The raised bath, with spectacular views over the city and harbor, is her preferred place for making unhurried telephone calls. 完

70

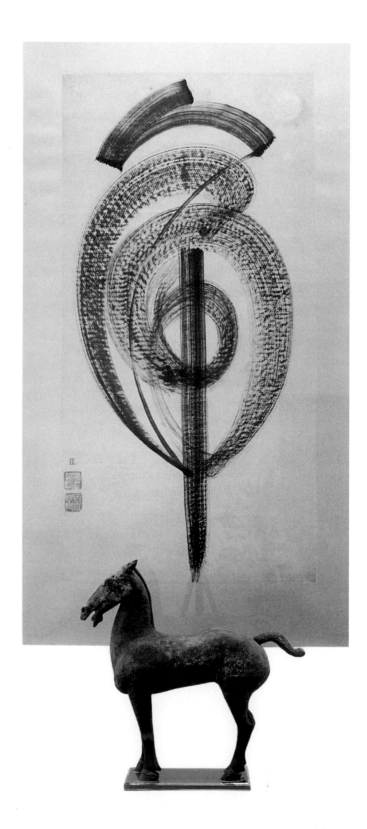

LEFT *The living room is cream in deference to the collection of art and artifacts: a 1953 bird sculpture by Bancel, a contemporary French wrought-iron sculpture by Hamisky, and pictures by Cecil Howard. The various works by French artists are to be expected, given Yan's nationality. He arrived in Hong Kong in the 1980s to work for L'Oréal, and now runs his own business.*

ABOVE *Wooden floors and ceiling fans throughout the house are original. The Ching Dynasty elmwood bed is an unusually large example. The Perspex-framed painting is by Nicole Dufour, a contemporary French artist.*

OPPOSITE *Another Nicole Dufour painting and a 12th-century Khmer torso can be contemplated from the bath.*

INDIAN RHAPSODY

印式体验

THIS IS A FAMILY HOME in the broadest sense: 50 relations live here under the same roof. To the visitor it seems more like a hotel, with 8 apartments in one block, another 30 rooms for offspring in an added wing, and public areas for frequent functions and Sunday evening family dinners. There is a cinema, a prayer room, and a gymnasium with a full-time masseur who is one of the 33 permanent staff. The duties of the housekeeper who oversees domestic affairs include drawing up dinner-party menus for up to 500 people with the aid of the house computer.

It all belongs to the Harilela dynasty, the most prominent, public, and respected Indian family in Hong Kong. The six brothers, whose father emigrated from Sind (now part of Pakistan) in the 1930s, have always lived together. They all work within the family empire, which encompasses hotels and restaurants worldwide, and trading, travel agency, and stockbroking operations. From their early days as silk retailers the Harilelas now run a multi-million-dollar enterprise.

The house was designed in 1967 by Dr. Hari Harilela, head of the family and a stalwart of public service in business, education, and charity. He designed

OPPOSITE *On one of the two etched and gilded dining tables in the Mogul Room stands a Czechoslovakian crystal pitcher and cut glass from Germany.*

ABOVE *The Harilela home stands out from its neighbors in high-rise Kowloon. Its disciplined, geometrical exterior belies the ornamental artistry within.*

RIGHT AND OPPOSITE
*The Mogul Room, used at
least three times a week, seats
up to 40 people for dinner.
There are two dining tables,
each with its own sitting area.
All mirrors and tables are
etched in gold leaf.*

BOTTOM RIGHT *The brass
jalee work was copied from
the Taj Mahal, where similar
filigree partitioning is
rendered in marble. The
Russian malachite pedestal
dishes and the finely carved
jade ornamental piece are part
of a decorative display in the
Mogul Room.*

the 82,000-square-foot, low-rise compound in the heart of high-rise Kowloon, taking his inspiration from India's Taj Mahal and Fatehpur Sikhri. Stepping into the entrance hall is like entering the foyer of an opera house: it is clad in marble and mosaics and, four stories up, capped with a cupola of turquoise stones. An immense Bohemian crystal chandelier, its drops sparkling like a sun-kissed fountain, dominates the space.

To the right of the hall is the Mogul Room, the main entertaining chamber, with 32 carved and gilded arches. Dining chairs bedecked like thrones in red velvet are set around two carved and gilded circular glass tables, while lower versions of the same table design stand in the front two quadrants of this mammoth room, the centerpiece of which is an octagonal marble column.

The top three stories of the east wing constitute the heart of the home. Dr. Hari himself designed all the decorative schemes, including the spiral staircases and the magnificent chandeliers. His personal favorite, however, is the pearl-canopied bedroom that he had made out of strings of Mikimoto pearls as a surprise for his beloved wife.

完

BELOW *One of two private dining rooms where the Harilelas gather for Sunday supper. The walls are paneled with wood and the furniture is an eclectic mix of Indian and Chinese.*

RIGHT *An intricate Hindu mosaic and marble basin outside the Prayer Room, where family members go to pray each day.*

OPPOSITE *The central hallway opens up to the full height of the house. Suspended from the dome-shaped ceiling, inspired by an Indian palace, is a spectacular crystal chandelier. Glass doors lead out onto courtyards on either side.*

PRIVATE VIEW

美景独享

SHUNNING THE LIMELIGHT in an ordinary block in the thick of Hong Kong's residential district, this sixth-floor apartment houses an extraordinary collection of contemporary fine art belonging to one of the island's best loved and leading art dealers, Sandra Walters. The varied range of art in her collection represents a distillation of the many exhibitions she has held since her first show in Hong Kong in 1973. "I love to buy for myself as much as possible," confesses this American enthusiast. Her enthusiasm extends to compiling biographies of the artists she promotes and with whose work she has transformed this series of box rooms into a vibrant living space.

Sandra and her husband, Richard, are long-timers in Hong Kong; they came for a vacation in the 1960s and never left. Since then she has set up and run her own gallery and art consultancy, earning a worldwide reputation; introduced many Western artists to the Hong Kong market; raised the profile of local artists; and played a prominent role in raising the public's consciousness of art. Her preview soirées at Mandarin Oriental Fine Art always drew hundreds of guests through the

OPPOSITE *The large abstract canvas in the living room is by Hong Kong's foremost modern painter, Hon Chi Fun. Although he has emigrated to Canada, he was a pivotal figure in the development of contemporary Hong Kong art. Over the years Sandra has sold 40 of his paintings. The abstract Chinese brush painting on the right is by Hong Kong artist Hai Tien.*

ABOVE *Sculpture was initially slow to find its market in Asia, but it has now gathered a significant following of discerning collectors. The Taiwanese Ju Ming is one of the most widely admired sculptors and his works are much in demand. This piece in bronze is from his celebrated series capturing the grace of tai chi movements.*

81

RIGHT *Art has even infiltrated the bathroom, vying for space with utilitarian objects such as towels and toothbrush holders. Above the small fiberglass sculpture by the British craftsman Kenneth Armitage hang two pen-and-ink drawings,* Masked Ball *and* Salzburg Festival, *by the Italian Lucianna Arrighi.*

door and put dozens of red dots on the paintings. The epitome of charm and modesty, Sandra still prefers to describe herself as a "gallery personality rather than authority."

One of her favorite artists is the avant-garde Russian painter Chemiakin, whose strident canvases of abstract figures compel attention on the living room wall. When she introduced his work to Hong Kong in 1995, Sandra was well aware that the bold colors and distorted contours would not immediately appeal to the "more conservative market." But, she maintains, collectors will not learn to appreciate new work if they are never exposed to it. "If you give people the art they know," she says, "where do you go from there? They must learn, and I like to educate and encourage."

Most of the art in the apartment is by contemporary Chinese artists, including Liu Shau Kwan who was master of the Chinese contemporary ink school and teacher of most of the current foremost Hong Kong painters.

In less talented hands the diversity of styles on display could have created an air of confusion, but Sandra's flair for hanging—and choice of neutral

decor—ensure an ambience of complete concord. Even the bathroom, a cabin of black marble and cream, contains works of art, such as the sculptures on display among the toothbrushes.

Next door in the bedroom is where the couple spend a lot of time working and relaxing before retreating to their favorite spot of all: bed. It is raised up from the floor to make the most of the stunning view over the high rises to the harbor. And in a city where neon knows no bounds, bedtime is the very best time for views. 完

ABOVE AND LEFT *The couple's bed is raised on a platform so that they can sit up and enjoy the "fabulous" view through the window.* Courtesans, *by the mainland Chinese painter Zhu Xin Jian, hangs above the bed. Jian emigrated to France, where he was allowed to paint subjects like these that were forbidden in China during the Cultural Revolution.*

LEFT *Detail of a painting by the Shanghainese artist Walasse Ting. He has lived in America and Holland but as a young man studied in Paris, where he fell in love with the work of Matisse. He added "sse" to his name out of respect for his hero.*

BELOW *In the guest bedroom, an early study on the Buddha image by Hong Kong artist Hai Tien.*

OPPOSITE *The paintings in the dining room are by the Shanghainese artist Chen Jialing. They demonstrate a contemporary interpretation of the age-old Chinese tradition of brush painting.*

ABOVE *The two vivid canvases are by the Russian artist Chemiakin, whom Sandra introduced to Hong Kong in 1995—the same year in which Chemiakin became the first living artist to have an exhibition at the Hermitage in St. Petersburg.*

A BEAUTIFUL OBSESSION

美丽的渴念

"IF I CAN'T SLEEP AT NIGHT I get up and look at them; it's an obsession," says Kai-Yin Lo of her impeccable collection of Ming Dynasty furniture, antiquities, and decorative objects. It ranked among the finest collections in Hong Kong before most of it was dispatched, on loan, to the Museum of Civilization in Singapore for safe keeping in the anticipation of uncertain years following the handover to Chinese rule. She would rarely go out on a Saturday evening, preferring to stay home and read up on the treasures she had spotted on her habitual weekend wander down Hong Kong's famous antiques row, known as Hollywood Road.

Kai-Yin became a passionate collector and an authority on the still little-documented tradition of Ming furniture after her return home to Hong Kong from years of study at England's Cambridge and London universities, when she found she missed the cultural side of life she had enjoyed in Europe. Her collecting began with decorative pieces in coral, ivory, and agate, and small jade carvings, which drew her into her career as a jewelry designer—now internationally renowned. Kai-Yin still wears some of her trademark pieces, instantly recognizable by their

OPPOSITE *The antiquity of a Han Dynasty terra-cotta horse and rider, originally a tomb icon, contrasts with the modern skyline beyond.*

LEFT *Sung Dynasty pottery (960–1279), recognizable by its shadowy blue-green hue, marks the beginning of porcelain in China; it has come to light during the past 15 years thanks to advances in excavation methods.*

size and their fusion of Eastern sensibility with Western aesthetics.

Time away from her drawing board (she now incorporates semiprecious and precious stones in more modern designs) and from the management of her 16 retail outlets worldwide sees Kai-Yin in avid pursuit of her latest obsession. As a Chinese educated abroad she felt frustrated by her inability to understand her country's traditional art. "I felt I represented a condition of many people in Asia. Because of our education we are not equipped with the literature,

87

RIGHT *This painting of the Grand Canyon shows how Wu Guanzhong absorbed what was going on outside his own sphere of influence. The pair of late-18th-century clothing chests are made from yu mu wood, inlaid with burl.*

BOTTOM RIGHT *Kai-Yin's passion for Ming furniture has a strong scholarly slant. She has a copy of nearly every book on the subject, housed here in rattan-and-matting cupboards.*

the philosophy, poetry, and calligraphy essential for the study of Chinese painting. I wanted to understand and I wanted other people to learn also."

This yearning led her to become the pivotal figure in the organization of the British Museum's first exhibition of work by a living artist, Wu Guanzhong, in 1992. While Kai-Yin had to drag the critics through the door then, she was delighted with the deluge of positive criticism that greeted the museum's subsequent show, Twentieth Century Chinese Painting: Tradition and Innovation, which she also sponsored. In 1996 the exhibition traveled from Hong Kong to London and Cologne. "Forget about China's economic prowess," noted the *International Herald Tribune*. "The greater Chinese miracle, when looked at by the cultural historian, is the renaissance of its age-old art, painting, now rising to heights unsuspected by the outside world."

Through her infectious enthusiasm for the art of China, Kai-Yin Lo has been instrumental in bringing it to the attention of a global audience. "I told the British Museum it was about time the West knew what has been happening in Chinese painting since the Communist regime took over." 完

OPPOSITE *The two paintings by the Beijing artist Wu Guanzhong reveal how traditional Chinese painting has been transformed from a spent force into one of the most exciting stories in contemporary world art, thanks to its confrontation with Western models that acted as catalysts in the evolution of a new style.*

OPPOSITE AND ABOVE *Kai-Yin Lo's enviable talent for
decoration is here applied to her dining table, a 19th-century
elmwood example, inlaid with ivory. Glassware is from Murano
and Prague; pottery and lacquerware (dark green instead of red
on the underside of rice bowls proves their 18th-century origins)
are from Japan; and the embroideries, sandwiched between
Perspex to make placemats, are from 19th-century China.*

LEFT *Kai-Yin describes this as "the most beautiful writing table on earth," and there is no other known example with the same particular folding method, even though generic folding tables appeared early in Chinese history when life was conducted at floor level. This Kang example (16th–17th century) has beautiful cabriole legs and outward-curving hoof feet.*

OPPOSITE *Lovingly laid out on a miniature display table is one of Kai-Yin's most cherished collections. She began collecting these Buddhist knots of destiny, made of ivory, wood, and mother of pearl, in the 1970s.*

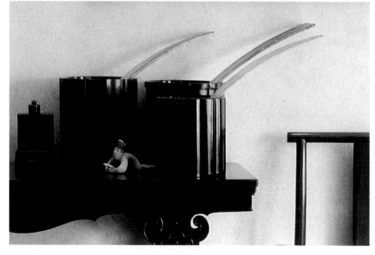

ABOVE *A detail of a rare jichi mu lute table from the 18th century. Its decorative style—the "horse belly drop" apron, the beading, and the Ruyi cloud decoration in the spandrels and knees—make this a pedigree example of the Palace Style. On the table are three brush pots and ivory spatulas carried by messengers at the Ming court.*

RIGHT *A collection of antiquities: (from left) a Boddhisatva (disciple of Buddha) from the Northern Qi period (550); a Pakistani Gandava head from the civilization of Alexander the Great; a Buddhist disk denoting heaven; and a Khmer torso dating from the 10th or 11th century.*

COOL CUSTOMERS

冷静的顾客

DESIGNER PETER HUNTER enjoys talking flippantly about his interior aesthetic, which, pure and simple—much like his interiors themselves—is cream and beige. He will often quote Bette Midler's line in the movie *Get Shorty.* When she walks into Gene Hackman's house she shrieks: "My favorite color: putty!" It is fitting that he chooses a line from a movie to convey his style, for in the past he has worked on residential projects for David Lean and Richard and Lily Zanuck.

Another favorite word in Peter's vocabulary is "taupe." If a prospective client wants a colorful home he will direct them swiftly elsewhere, for color, in his book, is far too stimulating to live with and one grows tired of it. He himself has always lived in a white-on-white interior. But he knows he would soon go out of business if he did not bend his rules a little when designing commercially, especially in a city not known for understatement.

Like much of Peter's work, the design for this 3,000-square-foot apartment, for a Japanese-Malaysian couple, focuses more on architecture than on pure decoration, resulting in connecting spaces that are calmly luxurious.

OPPOSITE *This is the finest room in the apartment because of the view it affords down the thick wooded hillside on the south side of Hong Kong island. The floor is laid with pale travertine, the soft stone with which much of Rome was built.*

LEFT *The gentle curves of an earthenware vase contrast with the strong vertical lines of a Ching Dynasty table.*

LEFT *Soft furnishings by the Parisian designer Philippe Hurel, based on styles by Jean-Michel Frank, were chosen for their simple monumentality. The mirror behind the shelves gives an illusion of space.*

ABOVE *A view into the living room from the hallway. The venetian blinds and the long shelves beyond emphasize the horizontal effect and draw the eye toward the window and the memorable vista.*

RIGHT *Much of the wall space is paneled in limed oak: "It's the nearest thing you get to beige in woods," says Peter. This hallway demonstrates Peter's trick of placing doors opposite doors (he does the same with windows). In this way all four corners of the apartment can be seen when standing at its center and the open, light nature of the layout is enhanced.*

In view of his emphasis on form, Peter says that color and what he terms "clutter" would detract from the consistency of the whole. Immediately upon entering this oasis of calm, the visitor senses an aura of order. The long "runway" carpet, the pelmet that supports the light fittings, the low furniture and shelves, and the venetian blinds have purposely been positioned to detract from any sense of verticality. They lead the eye to the focal point of the home, which is the picture window looking out over the south side of Hong Kong island. For the owners, this view down the wooded hill to the sea is the apartment's most important feature, and in the evenings their favorite place to relax is on the sofa next to the window, watching the sunset.

Having moved from a family home where they had brought up their three children, Peter's clients wanted something a little more sophisticated. Their brief required a place that was as open and simple as possible with a feeling of spaciousness. Thanks to the uniformity of color, the architectural format, and the materials used (limed oak and pale travertine stone), this apartment is more a mapping of interlocking spaces than a warren of rooms. Standing midway down the corridor in the center of the home, one has a viewpoint into every room.

Thrilled with the minimalism of their new abode, the owners now appreciate how it relaxes them when they come home from stressful jobs in trading. Their changed view of aesthetics has even influenced the wife's wardrobe, steering her toward Armani in neutral colors. "They have become more minimalist than me," jokes Peter. Nevertheless, he remains a master of interiors of the utmost integrity, where modernism melds with monasticism. 完

TOP RIGHT *The long strip of carpet, known to Peter and his clients as the "runway," links the various rooms that constitute the main living space. It was laid with expert precision so that it sinks flush with the stone floor under the weight of feet. The pelmets are a design trick to disguise the varying heights of windows and doors in the original construction. Together with the carpet they emphasize the room's horizontal nature.*

BOTTOM RIGHT *The juxtaposition of the old Ching-style robe rack with the contemporary dining arrangement is an intentional statement. Peter designed the dining table and coffee tables in an "absolutely no-design" form so as not to detract from the more dramatic furniture in the room.*

BELOW *The simple elegance of this Ming Dynasty table is reiterated in more contemporary pieces.*

OPPOSITE *Peter was commissioned for this project on the strength of his opinions on bathrooms, which the clients read in a newspaper article. "It's a sitting room with plumbing, the only place where you can be really private," he says of the favorite room in the home.*

FIRM FAVORITE

银行家的热门点

ON NEW YEAR'S EVE, 1894, in the glowing lamp-light of the German Club in Shanghai, a partnership was planned by two young Europeans. Over the century that has followed, the fruits of their labors and management foresight have contributed significantly to the shaping of Hong Kong into a nerve center for business and trade in Asia. Their fledgling enterprise, Jebsen & Co., began by operating 14 steamers in the China Coast trade, transporting Chinese wares. Unlike some of its rivals, it never traded opium, labeled "foreign mud" by the Chinese because it was imported from Bengal.

Hans Michael became chairman of Jebsen & Co. when he was 30, following in the footsteps of his grandfather Jacob, the founder, and he fully intends to pass on the still private family company to its fourth generation. He curtailed a degree in business administration in Denmark to join the ranks in 1981 when he was just 23, and ever since then his dynamism and business acumen have ensured Jebsen & Co.'s continuing expansion in international trade throughout Asia.

In view of the company's prospects (in 1996 it had 12 joint ventures with China), Hans Michael and

OPPOSITE *The pattern for the gallery in the living room was copied from a gallery in the house of Hans Michael's mother. Most of the soft furnishings were flown in from Europe to achieve authenticity.*

ABOVE *Apart from the columns, the exterior is a fine tribute to Macanese colonial architecture, with such elements as shutters, color, and pediments inspired by the Portuguese resort town of Sintra, near Lisbon.*

LEFT *Pedimented and pilastered bookcases and door frames throughout the house were crafted in China out of teak, while the* faux-marbre *columns were created by a paint-effects specialist from the U.K. The gallery leads to the guest wing.*

OPPOSITE *Hans Michael set out to replicate the style of houses he grew up in as a child in Denmark, his keen interest in architecture and design equipping him to mastermind the construction and decoration of his new Hong Kong home.*

featuring a baronial black-and-white marble hallway, double wooden doors, racing green in the study, and a marble fireplace in the dining room.

Furnished with chintzes, antiques, and classical history paintings, the main living room is circled above by a gallery to add dimension and provide a means of access to the guest wing. Elements of country house living are everywhere: a roaring fire in the grate, a grand piano, and regiments of silver-framed family photographs. While much of the design and color scheming was drawn up by Hans Michael himself, the couple also called upon the creative expertise of Ina Lindemann, a friend and interior designer from London, where many of the fabrics and paints were sourced.

Attention to detail has been meticulous. Hans Michael will proudly point to the deep bevel on the panes of glass in every window and the brass doorknobs, cast in China from a Danish design. Yet despite its relative grandeur this is very much a family home where dogs and children play. Hans Michael hopes that one day his two sons will not only lead the company well into the next century but also cherish the family seat that he has created.　　　完

his wife, Desiree, decided to settle in Hong Kong, and over three long years they built their family dream home from scratch. Its yellow colonial façade is easily spotted jutting out from the hillside on the south side of the island. Inside, the traditional theme is continued so convincingly that visitors could well believe they were stepping into a Georgian mansion in the English countryside. While their house in Europe displays ancestral arts and furniture from the Orient, as if by a trade-off their home in Hong Kong is decorated according to European tradition,

TOP LEFT *The balustrade of the garden wall curves around the swimming pool.*

BOTTOM LEFT *An Elysian vista of the south side of the island, overlooking Aberdeen.*

BELOW *The imposing dimensions of the front door are appropriate for such a stately residence.*

OPPOSITE *The façade is a paraphrase of the house built in 1890s Hong Kong by Jacob Jebsen, a founding partner of Jebsen & Co. and grandfather of the current chairman, Hans Michael. In 1914 that house was expropriated from the family, never to be returned. Instead the Jebsens received £1,500 in 1920, the statutory compensation for all "unfriendly nationals" after World War I.*

OPPOSITE *The European-style dining room looks out over the hills to the seething conurbation of Aberdeen, world-famous fishing port and trading center. The dining table can seat 24 guests, softly illuminated by a magnificent French fire-gilded chandelier from the 1890s.*

ABOVE *A tented anteroom in the guest wing, with walls covered in a fine fabric of bold teal and fine gold stripes. The pelmet and ornate drapes echo those in the dining room.*

ABOVE *When working in the racing green study, Hans Michael can gaze out through deeply beveled French doors to the inviting terrace beyond.*

RIGHT *Green leather cases fit snugly beneath a banquette in the study. One of many leatherbound family photograph albums lies open on top.*

OPPOSITE *A guest room decorated with hand-painted wallpaper by Zuber in France; the Napoleonic sleigh beds and silk fabrics are all from England.*

COUNTRY LIFE

绿色生活

SHEK O, ON HONG KONG'S southeastern tip, is the last bastion of pastoral living on the island. High-rise blocks have not ousted the gracious estate of houses like this one, which are mapped down the hillside leading to the village itself. A colonial measure passed in 1921 enabled the founding of the Shek O Golf and Country Club, and the government parceled out the adjoining stretch of land for the construction of 50 weekend bungalows. The advent of the Depression after World War I meant only 23 were finished before the building permits expired.

This house, on a 3.5-acre site, is now a Jardine Matheson property valued at roughly HK $200 million in 1996. It was built by the Wallem Shipping Company in 1926 and is widely regarded as the heart of Shek O, according to its current resident, Marie Terry. For during the 1949 revolution in China the house became the secret meeting place for leaders of the great "Hong" companies, and vital strategic decisions, such as Jardine's exit from Shanghai at the time, were made there.

After four phases of renovation it is now a family home (with seven dogs and singing birds), always open to the people of Hong Kong for business

OPPOSITE *At the back of the house the veranda overlooks a garden filled not with flower beds but with more than 200 flowering pots.*

ABOVE *One of the two full-time gardeners who water the pots twice a day and nurture 400 poinsettia plants for Christmas each year.*

113

OPPOSITE *Shek O village was hit hard by the Japanese during World War II because of its strategic position on the island. The house was occupied and stripped of everything except this hardwood paneling on the stairs and landing.*

RIGHT *The dining room is used for entertaining two or three times a week. Marks from champagne corks are still visible on the ceiling, evidence of occupation by employees of a Norwegian shipping company, who were known to have held wild parties here.*

or charity functions. "The house is not mine, I am just its steward for now," says Marie. In the summer more than 500 people a month have been known to picnic on its lawns and swim in its pool—some of them local children who have never walked on grass before.

Previous occupants had created four box rooms within the original one-bedroom bungalow, but by knocking down false ceilings and walls the Terrys have made one large and lofty living room. This main area leads to a covered terrace, where the family spend much of their time. Sitting on the veranda, with not another building in sight, it is hard to believe one is in Hong Kong. Marie bedecks the terrace with hanging lanterns and fairy lights depending on the time of year.

The garden is a celebration of color and scent, with crowds of flowers jostling for position—not in earthbound flower beds but in a flotilla of pots that can be redeployed to create a different scene, and also speedily moved at the first sign of a typhoon. Elsewhere in the garden are a duck pen, a vegetable plot, a swimming pool, and a stable block that the Terrys converted into apartments for their servants.

Back inside, the yellow decorative scheme is continued into the dining room, which is used for dinner parties on up to three nights a week. This room could also be said to double as an aviary because it houses the couple's eyecatching collection of ceramic parrots, which now numbers nearly 150. "We started collecting them because Greg's home country [Australia] is a parrot paradise," Marie explains. "We buy them wherever we see them around the world. They are not worth very much, but it gives us a lot of fun." 完

ABOVE *Part of Greg's unique flock of ceramic parrots.*

TOP LEFT *A collection of Tang Dynasty ceramic figures.*

LEFT *This copy of a Japanese Edo screen was bought from a local gallery for sentimental reasons: Marie's daughter, an artist, once did a series of paintings on fans.*

OPPOSITE *When the Terrys took up residence in 1993 they removed false partition walls and ceilings to restore the living room to its former lofty proportions.*

STYLE COUNSEL

风格指引

AFTER THE ROLEX, the Armani ensemble, and the chauffeur-driven car came the interior designer—and in particular Simon Jackson. He arrived in 1989 fresh from Australia and encountered a city hungry for a home with "hanger appeal"—plenty of clothes storage space. One opportune break and job very well done propelled him into Hong Kong's monied elite and almost overnight he became the designer everyone wanted to employ. He hasn't looked back since. Consistently high standards on projects for such gold-card clients as Goldman Sachs, New World Investments, and Cathay Pacific Airways have kept him on a professional pedestal, while his urbane manner and suave sartorial style have made him a social star and sustained his high profile year after year.

Although he has little time to spend at home, he has still managed to bestow his expert eye on his own apartment, furnishing it with art and antiques. "I believe my taste is more sophisticated now," he says. "It's been a natural process with my increased exposure to the world at large." His favorite form of shopping is at international auctions, where he has bought a string of objects once owned by celebrities, as well as some of his most exquisite furniture.

OPPOSITE *Simon's dining chairs were once owned by Barbra Streisand, while his crested and gilded dinner service originally belonged to Imelda Marcos.*

ABOVE *After nine years in Hong Kong, Simon says that his taste, opulent and eclectic, has also become more refined with time and exposure to a wider range of art forms.*

LEFT *This semainier, or seven-drawer chest, with its imitation Boulle marquetry, dates from circa 1855. Simon bought it at auction in New York to house his extensive collection of colorful neckties.*

OPPOSITE *Simon's flat shows a preponderance of gold, tassels, male nude paintings, and rich textures and fabrics in the French baroque style. The oil painting is by Arthur Boyd, a leading contemporary Australian artist.*

As a self-confessed fashion aficionado and shopaholic, Simon's favorite corner of the apartment is his bedroom-cum-dressing room, which is bigger than his drawing room. "I often buy duplicates of a piece of clothing that I like," he says, pointing to the wall-to-wall wardrobes with neat lines of shoes laid out on the carpet in front.

Although he says there was no blueprint that dictated the decoration of his apartment, there is an overall mantle of opulence and high style. For instance, a fine specimen of a Louis XVI dining

chair has been richly gilded, its seat upholstered with a floral tapestry fabric, and its back covered in bright turquoise damask. On reflection, Simon reveals that his love of gold, leopard skin, and rich textures is a reaction against the concrete and minimalism that surrounded him in 1980s Australia, when anything "modern and fascist" was considered de rigueur. Living in Hong Kong has made him question everything he thought before.

He now adores buying beautiful things: paintings, carpets, clocks from all periods and countries. Loyal to his birthplace, he cherishes his collection of 14 originals by Donald Friend, the renowned Australian artist. "I think I should put the brakes on and decide what I really do like, but I don't think I could do that. That sums me up: I believe my taste changes with time," he says. One thing remains unchanging, though—his quest for quality in everything from ties to tables.

However, there is no change when it comes to Simon's consistently high standards of decoration for prestigious clients such as Goldman Sachs (Asia) Limited, Renaissance Hotels International Inc., and Cathay Pacific Airways Limited. 完

TOP LEFT AND BOTTOM *A gold St. Nicholas icon hangs above a Regency ebonized and ivory-mounted klismos chair that Simon bought at auction in New York. The row of cream shoes—overspill from the wardrobe—is matched by a line of brown pairs on the opposite side of the room.*

OPPOSITE *Simon's dressing room is larger than his bedroom—a suitable solution for a fashion victim who duplicates when buying new shoes out of sheer forgetfulness.*

BELOW *A heavily carved Ching Dynasty chair in zitan wood.*

POTTED HISTORY

盆的历史

FEW WOULD BELIEVE that a quiet, leafy garden could exist amid the regiments of tower blocks in central Hong Kong. But there it undeniably is: the only private garden in the heart of the city, according to its owner and protector, Richard Tang, hidden behind the Art Deco apartment block in Happy Valley, where he lives.

"Money cannot buy this," says Richard, savoring the peace he feels as he wanders along its paths. The only noises are the splash of trickling water and the breeze rustling the branches of the trees. Otherwise there is a holy silence, perhaps all the more spiritual because this is a bonsai garden, combining art, history, and gardening, and thereby imbued with a particular beauty and tranquillity.

The garden's layout has been formulated to absolute precision on three distinct layers, joined by snaking pathways and steps cut into the slope of a hill. More than 200 bonsai trees, varying in strain and size, have been neatly positioned over the entire area, the tending and training of which require two full-time gardeners as well as the watchful eye of the old gardener who originally created the garden. The appearance of this, the only private bonsai garden in

OPPOSITE *A ceramic sculpture of a Chinese dragon stands guard in the garden. Despite its fearsome aspect, it is believed to symbolize power and good fortune.*

ABOVE *An avenue of 15 identical bonsai marks the second tier of the garden. It is natural for trees placed in tight groves like this to grow most of their leaves at the top to form a shared canopy.*

A menagerie of ceramic animals, including these cockerels, coexists peacefully among the clusters of bonsai. The bottom tier of the garden is lined with craggy rock, brought specially from China to recall the divine mountain areas of the mainland.

"cultivation"). The trees are cultivated and skillfully trained by wiring and pinching the branches to create the art forms for which bonsai are renowned. The height and shape of a bonsai are crucial. "You have to create the feeling of looking at a beautiful painting, and you only learn how to cultivate a bonsai by looking and learning with experience," says Richard.

The first bonsai cultivators tried to mimic the shapes that the trees would have acquired had they been buffeted by nature, and their shapes were meant to represent some aspect of the natural world—a sweep of a branch suggesting the curve of a cliff or a craggy mountainside, perhaps. A bonsai may look like a veteran of years of struggle against elemental forces that have altered its form dramatically. Although the true age of a tree is less important than the appearance of age, some bonsai in the garden are more than 100 years old.

Statues of sages, Buddhas, and prophets, meditating beside the bonsai or in nooks among the rocks, enhance the garden's mood. Beyond the gates all is speed and bustle, but here ancient arboriculture has made an oasis of stillness and calm. 完

Hong Kong, has remained unchanged since it was created in 1952 by Richard's father, Sir S. K. Tang. "It was one of my father's hobbies and he passed it on to me," says Richard. "I want to keep it the same out of loving memory for him."

The garden's bonsai were mainly brought from China, long called the Mother of Gardens because of the country's age-old tradition of creating sanctuaries for rest and spiritual refreshment. Translated loosely from the Japanese, bonsai is the art of growing plants in pots (*bon* means "tray" or "bowl", *sai* means

RIGHT *Man-made terraces carved into the garden's slopes provide an ordered backdrop for the venerable bonsai.*

BELOW *Zebras and pandas are other members of the garden's ceramic menagerie.*

BELOW *All true bonsai are planted in individual pots, carefully chosen to be a harmonious part of the artistic endeavor. Containers should be plain and simple so as not to detract from the artistry above. This brigade of bonsai is elevated on traditional Chinese stools and pedestals in the shady top level of the garden.*

RIGHT *Small ceramics of sages, like these two wise men reading scrolls and talking, are placed under the gnarled trunks of many of the bonsai, purely for decoration.*

OPPOSITE *A view of the tiered garden, with the traditional Chinese tea house built for shady respite in the heat of the day.*

ABOVE LEFT *The bountiful Chinese goddess of goodness, Guanyin, sits contemplatively among the garden's rocks.*

ABOVE RIGHT *This striking bonsai was trained to grow in a human form; a ceramic head was added to complete the effect.*

QUALITY STREET
特式街

IF ANY HOME in Hong Kong signifies the ultimate in sumptuous living, this is it. No expense has been spared in creating this magnificent residence for a Chinese family at the pinnacle of international society. Where many of us would have to resort to clever techniques to give the impression of quality, this family has bought the real thing. Four kinds of gold leaf embellish the molded dining room ceiling, precious stones are studded into door and cabinet pulls, and rooms are paneled in solid beech.

According to the designer, his clients are "connoisseurs of good food, good wine, and good living," and they wanted their home to reflect this. In view of this the main salon on the ground floor has been decked out as a private entertainment room for after-dinner relaxation, such as singing karaoke and smoking cigars. It is fitted with state-of-the-art video equipment, ingeniously disguised in the central coffee table and able to project images on to a screen that glides down over the painting at the far end of the room. The air-conditioning system is so sophisticated that the lighting up of the first cigar triggers its smoke-filtering mechanism. Sweeping bow windows offer a panoramic view of Deepwater Bay.

OPPOSITE *The private dining room, resplendent with gold leaf, bronze, and polished black granite.*

LEFT *A peek into the guest bathroom behind a solid beech door, made by the designer.*

The dining room, which is used for private entertaining at least three times a week, is a showcase of tasteful opulence. In addition to the gold leaf on the ceiling and chairs, the inlaid wooden table is supported on cast-bronze legs and the floor is of polished black granite. Outside stands an elegant altar table bearing the vintage wines to be served at dinner.

The distinctive flair of the interior designer has been allowed to flourish untrammeled here. However, convenience has not been sacrificed to style; an elevator, with gold-plated doors, has been

installed to service each of the three floors. The only other restrictions placed on the design of the interiors were those imposed by feng shui considerations. It took months to align the rooms and their contents in the most fortuitous positions for sustained wealth and good fortune.

Despite the grandeur of each room, an inviting softness pervades the whole interior—just as the owners requested. This is doubtless a result of the alliance between the best natural materials and an experienced design eye.

ABOVE AND OPPOSITE *Much thought was given to ensuring that the bedroom belonging to the only child in the family is a playtime paradise. A painted ceiling, lots of space, and toys galore provide endless scope for exciting games and escape into a fantasy world.*

完

LEFT AND BOTTOM LEFT *The walls of the main vestibule have been decorated in a Venetian plaster finish to evoke an atmosphere of hallowed splendor. The reproduction Egyptian throne chair was bought at auction. The only thing lacking is a pharaoh or a doge.*

BELOW *A winding inlay of white granite marks out a path from the elevator doors to the dining room.*

OPPOSITE *A view into the main lobby area from the private entertainment room. The exquisite torchères were specially commissioned from the British designer Mark Brazier-Jones, who made the lanterns out of colored quartz and rock instead of glass. The table is also by Brazier-Jones.*

135

ABOVE *The master bedroom is a beautiful boudoir of dreamy creams and beiges. All the fittings were specially made for the room.*

LEFT *Lacquered banisters adorned with gold leaf have been taken from the grandparents' house, which shares the same plot on the hillside.*

OPPOSITE *This dressing table is a one-off design meant to evoke the mood of a Hollywood dressing room.*

THE COLOR OF MONEY

钞票本色

AT THE END OF THE 1980s Hong Kong was in the grip of what interiors writers have called an "interiority complex." Every self-respecting socialite's must-have accessory was her interior designer, and life was not complete without her own rotunda, marble floors, and chandeliers. This sweeping trend was sparked by Hong Kong's newly opened Grand Hyatt hotel, whose lavish lobby remains one of the most talked-about in the world. After the Hyatt came this 16,000-square-foot triplex and its designer, Simon Jackson, who set the local residential interiors scene on a new trajectory.

When the triplex was completed the resident billionaires, who own a significant international hotel and property portfolio, held a house-warming party. It appeared that people had received the message: they wanted the same and they wanted to say that Simon Jackson had designed their homes for them. It seemed to add certain prestige. Simon, a talented Australian who reflects that his rise to the position of Hong Kong's most wanted designer has been "quite amazing," was only 28 when he designed this imposing home under the auspices of his former firm. It was just a matter of weeks after his arrival that

OPPOSITE *The interior rotunda, reaching up three stories, adds heart-stopping grandeur to the interior scheme. Multilevel hanging crystal lamps are by Barovier and Toso, while the rest of the furniture was bought in London.*

ABOVE *Simon introduced Garouste and Bonetti to Hong Kong with chairs like this one bought in London.*

139

TOP RIGHT *The highlight of the lounge room is a fine French console, which had to be regilded because the client thought the original looked too dirty. The Russian contemporary painting above was bought by Simon Jackson from London's Raab Gallery.*

BOTTOM RIGHT *The whole interior was themed around the color of gold bullion. The sofas and coffee table were designed by Simon Jackson, while the Louis XVI chairs are reproductions, bought in Hong Kong.*

he won this contract. Now he runs his own consultancy, with many of Hong Kong's leading businessmen as clients.

In 1989, when Simon worked on this interior, people in Hong Kong wanted a Western-style home designed by a Westerner. Other than that the brief tended to be fairly loose, as long as clients felt they were getting value for money. Here, in one of the territory's largest apartments, this value translated into gilded furniture and marbled columns. Simon did everything. He went on shopping trips to New York and London and advised his clients on all choices of fabric and furniture. When it came to buying art, they trusted his taste. For his part, Simon has always believed that decoration should be a reflection of his clients' personality. "They must feel comfortable, and not embarrassed by an interior that they may not understand," he says.

Thus, with these particular clients in mind, he designed the whole scheme on a grand and impressive scale. Like a cupola in an Italian Renaissance church, the rotunda in the center of the apartment rises majestically through three stories, its marble-wash paint effect (with traces of copper) broken by

OPPOSITE *The double duplex is on the forty-fourth floor of Convention Plaza, Hong Kong's premier exhibition hall, which overlooks the harbor. It is flanked by the Grand Hyatt and New World Harbor View hotels. The whole complex is owned by the resident family.*

LEFT *These bonsai trees on marble columns studded with gold disks were included to add formality to the space and distract attention from the glass curtain wall.*

BOTTOM LEFT *This table and mirror in the family room were brought from New York. A brass model of a Japanese warship floats atop the table.*

OPPOSITE *The main stairwell links the four floors of what is reputed to be one of Hong Kong's largest homes. The marble stairs are covered with a leopard-print carpet.*

horizontal bronze bands. The floors and ceiling, inlaid with matching gold disks, are enhanced by the brilliant reflections cast by the Murano glass chandeliers, specially commissioned from Venice. All rooms leading off this pivotal center are equally imposing, like state rooms in a European palace; any sense of home has been banished, at the owners' request, in favor of formality.

Simon has cleverly adapted his austere interior scheme to complement the panoramic harbor views that take the breath away all around the apartment thanks to its position on the forty-third to forty-sixth floors of Hong Kong's most impressive harbor-front building. The glass facing provides floor-to-ceiling windows at every level, allowing light to flood the interior except in the stairwell area. Here Simon has masked the glass curtain wall with a construction of oversize portholes in order, he says, "to give strength to the space and to make the glimpses of view that much more dramatic."

This resourcefulness and originality, combined with his congenial and approachable personality, are doubtless what have gained Simon such respect among his clientele in Hong Kong. 完

LIVING BY DESIGN

精心的生活

WHEN WAILEE CHOW was planning to move out of her family house and set up home on her own, she had firm ideas about what she wanted. As an architect, now running her own practice, she was not going to settle for a series of box rooms in a high-rise apartment block. Her refusal to compromise entailed a lengthy search, and countless weekends were spent scouring Hong Kong for that old, unusual building that would set her creative juices flowing. She was in her early thirties when she finally found the perfect place: the last remaining block of a 1925 terrace with stained glass in the windows and high ceilings. A rare find indeed. "I knocked on the door to ask if it was for rent and was to told to come back in six months," she recalls. It was well worth the wait.

Wailee has now renovated the ground floor of this former family home, elevating it—metaphorically—into a New–York–style loft with just two rooms and an eclectic mix of signature pieces of furniture. Like many of her generation who have lived abroad (she studied in Bristol and Oxford, England), she says that her sense of interior style has been influenced by the different cultures she has experienced on her travels. "I like antiques because

OPPOSITE *Three monumental canvases by Campenelli, a young Italian architect, dominate the large living space. "I love them for their architectural feeling," says Wailee.*

ABOVE *A series of photographs by Willy Moy show the changing weather at Yellow Hill, a famous retreat in the heart of China where May was entranced by the landscape's moods.*

147

LEFT AND FAR LEFT *This delicate shagreen cabinet is a copy of an original (now in the Musée des Arts Decoratifs in Paris) by Iribe, who was designing furniture in the 1920s and 1930s. The Hong Kong furniture designer Garrison Rousseau is pioneering a new vogue for shagreen furniture, made with dyed stingray skin.*

ABOVE *Wailee's much-loved grand piano dictated the attributes that any potential new home had to possess: not only would it need to be large enough to house the piano, it had to have good acoustics—not something that home hunters often make a point of looking for. The ceilings here are 16 feet high.*

RIGHT *This rough-hewn glass chair was created by the British furniture designer Danny Lane, who has been a friend of Wailee's since school days.*

they are well made, well proportioned, and good value for money, but I have one or two modern things because they draw me back into the time I am in," she says, with reference to her Biedermeier and Baccarat, her Le Corbusier sofa, and her contemporary designer pieces.

She has cleverly ignored convention to suit her likes and her lifestyle. Her old-style bathtub, for example, is plumbed in at the foot of her bed because she adores taking baths, twice a day. "I do all my design when I am relaxed and soaking in the tub," she explains, remembering the bad old days when she had to share bathrooms with her brothers and sisters, who would knock on the door and hurry her out. "I hate the cold, and the tiles, and the smell of soap that bathrooms have." Now she simply rolls out of bed into the hot water, lights her candles, eats papaya, and does her thinking.

While cooking is Wailee's passion, she has not built a separate dining room, preferring instead to set out a series of little tables in her living room whenever she entertains. This room also houses her custom-made Bulthaup kitchen area with movable chests of drawers and glass-fronted cupboards and fridge.

Art is her second great love, and although she has an advisor to guide her when making additions to her collection, she is confident enough to follow her own feelings, too. "If I like it, and I can afford it, I buy it," she says. "I go by my instincts." Her collection consists predominantly of contemporary pieces by friends and mentors. Of all her artworks, though, perhaps her prize possession is a much-treasured canvas by the French painter Raoul Dufy. Reflecting on her taste, Wailee concludes, "This is me: I am between modern and classic." 完

149

ABOVE *Wailee's free-standing bathtub is literally at the foot of her bed,* "so that I can roll straight into it. I've never liked leaving my cozy bed to go into a cold, tiled bathroom."

OPPOSITE *Both stylish and practical, glass-fronted Bulthaup kitchen cabinets enable Wailee to find crockery, cutlery, and condiments in an instant when concocting her culinary masterpieces.*

ACE OF CLUBS

顶尖儿

SHE WAS ONLY BORN IN 1990, but she is already as much a part of Hong Kong's vocabulary as tram, taipan, or David Tang, her mentor and creator, a high-profile impresario who knows how to turn a concept into a reality. He certainly hit the jackpot with the China Club, which almost overnight became the hub of the Hong Kong elite's social life and an outstanding commercial triumph. "My clubs," he says, alluding also to the sister club in Beijing, "are a protest against the way Hong Kong and China are unknowingly drifting towards the West." So, here in Hong Kong at least, he took the theme of pre-revolutionary Shanghai, with all its nostalgia for teahouses and Art Deco flourishes, and injected it with a shot of funk: strong contemporary Chinese art, bold colors, and a mix of opulence and studied dilapidation. Just days before the grand opening David was spotted, hammer in hand, poised for the attack on surfaces in need of instant aging.

Characteristically, David dispensed with design consultants and bulk suppliers as much as possible and fashioned his club in his own image, doing the shopping and shifting the furniture until it looked right. Without his taste, flair, and genuine love, he

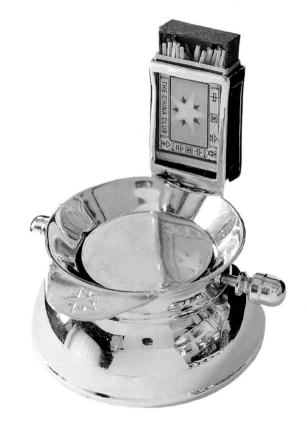

OPPOSITE *The China Club's balcony, once the scene of riots that fanned the Communist rebellion in Hong Kong in 1967, now stands in the shadow of the Citibank tower building.*

ABOVE *A reproduction of a 1930s silver-plated ashtray. They were specially commissioned by David Tang, to complement the prerevolutionary Shanghai theme of the private club.*

153

LEFT *David found the old leather sofa on the pavement outside White's Club in London. How fitting that the grandfather of gentlemen's clubs should bequeath part of its heritage to a young heiress in Hong Kong!*

BOTTOM LEFT AND OPPOSITE *The Long March Bar has a collection of Art Deco ware from Paris and stained glass from London. David personally hammered the bar top to achieve a distressed effect. Lace antimacassars hark back to the 1940s.*

would not have been able to recreate the China of the glossy pre-war Hollywood movies. "There was nothing theatrical in Hong Kong. Every fancy restaurant is in a fancy hotel with gold plate and marble everywhere. I wanted to build a place that was entirely comfortable and amusing," he declares.

In addition to Chinese antiques, there are plump armchairs in the signature colors of red and yellow, which create instant drama in the entrance hall. This leads to the splendid dining room, decked out with ceiling fans, red leather banquettes, marble-topped tables, and black wood chairs. A sweeping staircase, with elegant wrought-iron balustrades, winds up to the Long March Bar, a long lobby of a space in silver and frosted tones. Parlors, mahjong dens, and private dining rooms, laid out with the intimacy of a private home, lead the way to the top-floor library housing David's personal collection of 6,000 books on China and its people. This is not a club for the fitness freak. "If people want to exercise in a club they should be exercising their brains," says David, an avid reader. He does admit, though, that members like to point out the books to their guests proudly rather than sit quietly and read them.

OPPOSITE *The entrance hall typifies the mood of the whole club: a felicitous blend of English and Chinese styles that reflects David's Anglophile tastes and romantic yearning for Imperial China.*

LEFT *A set of ceramic figures from the revolutionary period depicting the Long March, after which the bar is named.*

BELOW *As visitors ascend the club's elegant stairwell they encounter an impressive collection of contemporary Chinese paintings, many of them portraits.*

The library overlooks the balcony, from where Communists fanned the flames of riot in 1967. Indeed the building itself is the former Bank of China and the de facto headquarters of the Chinese Communists in Hong Kong. "Ever since I was a child, before I went to live in England because of the riots, I have thought there was something mysterious about the top of this building . . . the home of senior cadres, thick with spies."

When he started on the China Club, his first big financial venture, David was determined to secure the top three floors of his favorite building. The former bank seemed to him the perfect premises to embody his Shanghai theme because it symbolized the juxtaposition between East and West that is Hong Kong.

Today no discerning celebrity visiting Hong Kong will leave before receiving an invitation to the China Club. 完

LEFT *David designed the banquette seating, in red leather and black wood, and added the stained-glass panel for visual amusement. The painting by the Chinese contemporary artist Chiu Ya Tsai recalls Modigliani.*

BELOW *Members and their guests are greeted by staff, dressed in red-trimmed, crisp white Mao-style jackets, from behind a stained-glass hatch.*

OPPOSITE *David's Anglophilia does not extend to the dining room, which serves only Chinese cuisine. Incredibly, each of the 180 dining chairs has a differently carved back panel and each was bought by David in China or Hong Kong.*

ABOVE *Each dining table is set out along the lines of a pre-war Shanghai teahouse. Etched-glass teacups and silver-plated chopsticks can be bought from the neighboring Shanghai Tang, the retail venture that David launched after the China Club.*

ALADDIN'S CAVE

亚拉丁的洞穴

THAI ARISTOCRAT HARRY Bunyarak has transformed a very insignificant flat in Hong Kong's Happy Valley into a veritable showcase for fine specimens of Asian art and antiques. It is hard to believe that his home is really just four small rooms, identical in layout to the millions of other apartments that run the stretch of the territory. It's also hard to believe that he has managed to collect such a wealth of beautiful objects all by the age of 28. But then he is fortunate to have grown up in a cultured family, surrounded by exquisite examples from the region's artistic past. He is convinced that it was this breeding ground that set him on his passionate hunt for classic Chinese furniture, Thai and Tibetan silver, and Asian contemporary art, his three main areas of interest.

Despite the tight squeeze for guests in the tiny dining room, Harry likes to throw dinner parties for the artistic elite. With scented candles flickering and night lights glowing, the setting is an Aladdin's Cave of visual delights and an alluring backdrop for Harry's tales from his anthology of collecting adventures. One of these concerns his Tibetan silver dealer, a hippy Dutchman from Lhasa

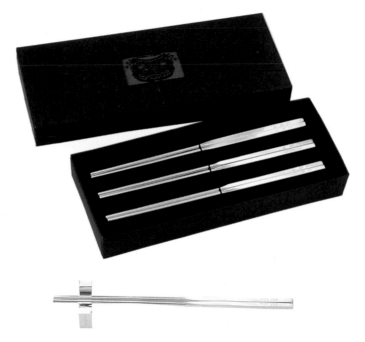

OPPOSITE *One bedroom was painted high-gloss, fire engine red as part of its transformation into a dramatic dining room with glass table and replica yoke-back Ming chairs, rusty gold Thai silk curtains and blue-and-white place settings, made for Harry to an ancient Chinese design by a Hong Kong factory.*

ABOVE *Silver-plated chopsticks, part of Harry's vast silver collection, add a touch of exoticism to traditional Chinese dining.*

LEFT *This corner of the living room displays Harry's collection of blue-and-white Ching porcelain, which he bought in bulk in Hong Kong for decorative, rather than investment, purposes. The painting, lit by candles, is an early figurative piece by Dao Hai Phong, one of his favorite Vietnamese artists.*

gold-leaf rattles, rings, broken bracelets, and shells that had been dug up by villagers while plowing their land. "Archaeology is not very sophisticated in parts of Thailand," he says.

Harry has turned his three-bedroom apartment into one bedroom plus a study, a dressing room, and a dining room in order to accommodate his precious collection and suit his lifestyle. Barely one inch of white wall is visible amid the collage of paintings that Harry also collects. He likes to steal the odd weekend to visit Hanoi and another dealer friend of his who has helped him develop his eye for quality. Mai, who runs her own Mai Gallery there, was one of the first to fuel the now-popular contemporary art movement in Vietnam. With her, Harry visits artists' homes and studios and buys directly from them. "I don't buy everything any more," he laments. "I focus on buying four or five really good pieces."

It's a blessing that Harry's career as a stockbroker is forcing him to move. He will definitely need a larger home if he sustains his current rate of collecting, which he fully intends to do. "I think I'll move on to collecting Old Master drawings," he muses. "They will go well with what I have already." 完

who always calls on Harry when he visits Hong Kong to sell to its top dealers. They first met in the Holiday Inn in Kathmandu when Harry was 16. He was on holiday with his parents and the dealer was selling silver from the next-door room. Harry has been buying from him ever since.

Then there's the tale of his four-day pilgrimage to Isarn in Eastern Thailand, where he had to bribe political rebels in order to visit the isolated 12th-century Khmer temples. He returned laden with boxes of Khmer artifacts such as tarnished bronze and

ABOVE *A pair of Ching Dynasty chicken-cage chairs grace the living room. Harry's exquisite collection of silver includes etched drinking cups and small beaten-silver shrines (carried when trekking) from Tibet, and bowls and betelnut boxes from Thailand.*

RIGHT *A bowl and plate from Harry's collection of blue-and-white porcelain. The pieces date from the Kangxi period (1662-1722).*

163

OPPOSITE *Harry had the desk in his study copied from a traditional Ming Dynasty design. Side by side with the Vietnamese art in this room are two pieces by Harry himself; a self-taught amateur, he is known to erect an easel and paint by the light of the moon when he feels inspired. The chair matches those in the dining room.*

ABOVE *In Harry's simply furnished bedroom the dark oil painting above the bed is an early work by Dao Hai Phong, which Harry bought direct from the artist during a personal visit to his apartment in Hanoi.*

RIGHT *A stained moon-lock cabinet in Harry's dressing room was refitted with slats to hold his shoe collection. Above hangs a painting of his niece and nephew by his French uncle.*

MODEL ELEGANCE

高雅的模式

FIRST IMPRESSIONS ARE that Beverly Hills has come to Hong Kong. This Art–Deco–style house is the only one of its type on the island and its photogenic quality made it a perfect setting for its former owner, the willowy model Sally Mount. She and her English husband, Duncan, sold the house in 1996 for HK $163 million (U.S. $20.8 million) in order to move to Boomerang, one of the most spectacular houses on the harbor front in Sydney, Australia. Five out of their seven years in the house were spent renovating—a job they had thought would take just a few months—proof that Hong Kong is more geared to demolition and construction than to refurbishment.

Although the finished house has that rarefied, cream-hued quality—as a backdrop for signature artworks and pieces of furniture—it remained very much a family home where young children pushed their plastic toys across the polished floor and scrabbled through the tunnel of dining chairs that encircled the massive marble dining table.

Throughout the 7,000-square-foot interior there is an indulgence of space to the extent that the hallway is larger than the dining room. Many of the

OPPOSITE *In the dining room a 9-foot slab of Veneziano marble was used as the top for a dining table. It is surrounded by 18th-century Italian dining chairs.*

ABOVE *A medieval-style cabinet by Mark Brazier-Jones, with curved legs molded to resemble coral.*

OPPOSITE *The magnificent entrance hall and sweeping staircase introduce visitors to the Art Deco style of the house. The hall table is by Nick Allen and the torchère by Mark Brazier-Jones.*

RIGHT *A contemporary console and mirror by Scott Cunningham, which harmonized with an 8th-century Cambodian bust, helped create the Pompeian mood of the guest bathroom.*

walls are bowed, echoing the generous curve of the spiral staircase with its wrought-iron banister in keeping with the Art Deco mood.

The palatial property was originally built in 1940 for Hong Kong's best known tycoon, Sir Run Run Shaw, who used it as a country house in the days before the Aberdeen Tunnel was cut through the mountain to link the south side of the island with the commercial north coast. In the intervening years it has been used as a movie location, complete with stuntmen shooting through its top-floor windows on motorbikes and landing in the bay beyond.

None of the furniture in the house is either diminutive or predictable. The couple's taste embraces an unusual combination of periods: namely 18th-century French, classical, and contemporary designer. The Mounts figured among Hong Kong's best patrons of Britain's leading living designers—Mark Brazier-Jones, Scott Cunningham, Nick Allen, Danny Lane, and William Walker—whose work is more generally bought by such taste shapers as Terence Conran, Madonna, and Mick Jagger. The dramatic furniture is effectively set off by polished wooden floors, cream carpets, and pale walls intermittently covered with murals (Egyptian in the bathroom and Capriccio-style in the dining room).

Fortune smiled on the house the day that Duncan and Sally became its owners. At one time this Art Deco house was scheduled for demolition—an act of vandalism too shocking to contemplate. On the Mounts' departure at the end of 1996 it achieved the highest recorded price ever reached at a residential property auction in Hong Kong. Thus was an architectural pearl mercifully saved for succeeding generations. 完

OPPOSITE AND TOP LEFT *In Duncan's dressing room Nigel Crawley painted a mural of Sally with a Harley Davidson. The sofa is by Scott Cunningham.*

BOTTOM LEFT *The decoration throughout the house was deliberately minimal so that the many signature pieces of furniture, such as this bed by Scott Cunningham, were displayed to maximum effect.*

BELOW *This metal wing chair is by British designer Mark Brazier-Jones, whose experimental and ornamental furniture made him one of the darlings of the style seekers in 1980s London.*

171

BELOW *The commissioned TV cabinet is by Mark Brazier-Jones, whose organic, ornamental designs spring less from any cerebral agenda than from a repertoire of ingredients in his memory bank. His work has found permanent homes in the Louvre and the Pompidou Centre in Paris.*

OPPOSITE *This view from the terrace outside the master bedroom shows how the feng shui for this house is perfect. The curve of the bay in front denotes security, the water means money, and the islands beyond prevent it from running away. Duncan's 17 years in Hong Kong made it impossible to ignore feng shui, which is why the family never used the front door, but came and went by a side door.*

ABOVE *In his student days Duncan would borrow his mother's car to visit country auctions around England. Now he buys from Sotheby's and Christie's such antique pieces as those seen here in the drawing room: a French provincial Louis XV sofa with 18th-century tapestry cushions and an 18th-century mirror and fireplace. The small coffee table is 1920s French.*

LEFT AND BELOW *The marble sunken bath is fit for Cleopatra. Sparkling windows, reflected in a wall of mirrors above the basins, provide illumination by day; hanging lanterns and wall lamps glow softly at night.*

OPPOSITE *An Egyptian theme was chosen for the bathroom, whose magnificent walls were designed and painted by Nigel Crawley. An ancient Grecian urn confers an element of authentic antiquity.*

HOUSE OF BULLION

金屋

AT HOME IN HONG KONG they are the most photographed couple. Abroad they are ambassadors for its social image. There can only ever be one Kai Bong and Brenda Chau, self-confessed socialites whose innocent pleasure in dressing up has earned them their reputation for fun-loving display. They regularly attend functions on at least four nights a week, and the pressures of starring on the social scene even forced Brenda to resign her job as a barrister in order to free her afternoons for sartorial preparation.

Having spent their student years in the 1960s on London's Carnaby Street, they claim to have introduced fashion to Hong Kong. "No one here had seen a mini skirt or a Brigitte Bardot hairstyle until Brenda returned home," Kai Bong asserts. Cross-dressing takes on a new meaning entirely when Kai Bong's waistcoat and tie are made from the same opulent fabric as his wife's ballgown, and the color-coding has even spread to their chauffeur, who wears a uniform of pink or gold depending on which Rolls-Royce he is driving.

The Chaus' imposing house, Villa D'Oro, sparkles in the sunset on the west side of the island.

OPPOSITE *The color of bullion is just for fun, says Kai Bong. This is one of two gilded table settings to be seen in the house.*

LEFT *The formal dining room is lined with gold except for the stained-glass mural along one wall, entitled "Flowers of All Seasons."*

It is hard to imagine any other home that so accurately reflects the personality of its owners. A homage to a passion for pink and gold, it is a flamboyant exercise in excess and a winner with the global media. Yet when the American *National Enquirer* magazine claimed that it was a more expensive residence than the White House, Kai Bong was outraged. "We are basically humble people," he declares. "We do not brag; we just consider ourselves artistic and we design things for fun." One example of this "artistic fun" is the wall of the "dessert" dining

177

OPPOSITE *At sunset the view across the channel from the garden room at Villa D'Oro is breathtaking.*

TOP RIGHT *Kai Bong and Brenda retreat to the Buddha Room on the top floor for contemplation when they return from socializing in the small hours. Its peace prepares them for sleep.*

BOTTOM RIGHT *The famous car that has earned Kai Bong and Brenda Chau their sobriquet of "The Pink Rolls-Royce Couple." The chauffeur wears a pink cap and dicky when driving it.*

room, which is covered in beads from one of Brenda's ballgowns, while her image is captured in a portrait made of pearls.

In both dining rooms all the crockery is gold or gold-dipped, including the shark-fin soup bowls that used to belong to Kai Bong's grandmother. Leading off the dining room—in a typically idiosyncratic departure from a conventional layout—the couple's bedroom is a gilded chamber of embroidered fabric and veneered wardrobes. The adjacent bathroom, the color of bullion, was painstakingly put together by Kai Bong and Brenda over many years, trips to Europe and to various Italian dealers in sanitary ware and swan-spouted taps, yielding the unusual features that now adorn it.

The top floor of the house is dedicated to the Buddha and to an impressive collection of Chinese jade carvings. Called the Buddha Room, this symphony in coral and gold is the couple's retreat in the small hours—they come here to pray and be peaceful on their return from social functions. Kai Bong generally retires to bed before his wife, who is known to stay up until dawn, then repair to her bed until lunch the following day.

Funds for the Chaus' fun-loving lifestyle have come from Brenda's family coffers in the Kowloon Motor Bus company; Kai Bong's late, knighted father; Kai Bong's property investments in Hong Kong and abroad; and his legal firm, which he set up after obtaining his master's degree from Cambridge University in England.

They have been so happy with the interior design of the house that with the passing of time the only things that have changed are the wardrobe dimensions and the size of the press clippings file. 完

BELOW *Kai Bong's father, the Hon. Sir Sik-Nin Chau, was presented with this gold pagoda by the Japanese Government.*

RIGHT *American gold coins adorn the guest bathroom—a characteristically quirky detail.*

FAR RIGHT *A portrait of Brenda Chau, made of Mikimoto pearls.*

ABOVE AND ABOVE RIGHT *In Brenda's dressing room even the taps and the telephone have not escaped the Midas touch.*

OPPOSITE *The formal dining room is lined with gold except for the stained-glass mural along one wall. The chandeliers were made in Taiwan to the Chaus' specifications, using imported crystal. The chairs are upholstered in springbok hide.*

JUNGLE HIDEAWAY

城市中的隐密处

THIS IS ONE OF THE MOST extraordinary homes in Hong Kong. That a large property built in 1925 still stands in the heart of the island's most densely packed residential area is remarkable in itself, but that its means of access is by steep wooded path, on foot or by golf cart only, is a startling anachronism in the archetypal modern city. But for residents Elisabetta and Peter Mallinson the approach adds to the delight of living in secluded jungle just three minutes' drive from the center of town. It doesn't bother them that it took two weeks to move in, that the postman will deliver only every other day, and that guests must be transported by buggy to the front door.

The house, which for 20 years was an English school, has escaped demolition because it was privately owned until one of Hong Kong's large developers made an offer of a lifetime. It is only a matter of time before the colonial property will be replaced by a health club or a high rise, but this has not deterred the English-Italian tenants from turning it into a temporary family home. Like many expatriates, the Mallinsons are used to moving house at short notice; they had to leave London very speedily when a leading investment bank sent Peter to Hong

OPPOSITE *The house is hidden in a rare stretch of jungle in a prime residential area. Birds, bats, and baby owls regularly find their way onto the garden patio.*

ABOVE *The imposing front gates at the end of the narrow path that winds 1,500 feet up from the nearest road. Moving in took two weeks and a team of 25 strong men.*

183

OPPOSITE *A dwarf-sized, 18th-century chaise longue. The nude painting is by the Post-Impressionist artist Bloomfield, who was a protégé of one of Elisabetta's forebears. She has six of his nudes, given to her by her grandmother, who found the subject matter too risqué.*

RIGHT *Much money and effort has been spent on the upkeep of the house, which is beautifully appointed inside with hardwood window frames and a teak floor. The front of the house opens up onto a balcony that wraps around the whole building on two levels.*

Kong just as they had finished refurbishing their new home there.

The couple have filled the tall, airy rooms of the house with Italian and British antiques, handed down from their ancestors. Thanks also to the colonial style of the place, visitors could be excused for thinking they were walking into a large London home, save for the beautiful pieces of Asian art that sit easily in the decorative scheme. The house is unusually large for Hong Kong, with its lofty entrance hall, three sitting rooms, dining room, and conservatory, all linked by polished teak floors and ground-to-ceiling wood-framed windows that open out on to a terrace skirting the circumference of the house just above the thick jungle fringe.

The terrace, cheerfully cluttered with pots of roses and tropical plants, is a favorite spot and weekends are spent entertaining outside in the dappled sunshine beneath the trees.

Italy is still very much at the heart of this home as Elisabetta grew up in Rome, but she enjoys the contrast that Hong Kong offers. As a professional picture restorer she was not expecting to work here, yet she found herself spending two years cataloging and restoring Jardine Matheson's corporate collection of 38 China trade paintings by two leading artists of the mid-19th-century genre: Chinnery and Lamqua. Pictures of trading vessels on the China coast were important topographical records before the advent of cameras, at a time when Jardines and others were shaping the economy of the region. Elisabetta spends quiet days working on these at her easel in the attic.

The couple go antique shopping every Saturday, both relishing the opportunity to diversify their European collection with Asian treasures. 完

OPPOSITE *Elisabetta's writing desk is flanked by a 19th-century Burmese lacquer-and-wood Buddha, known in the trade as a "Lady Buddha" because of its elegant proportions.*

ABOVE *The dining room boasts a limited-edition contemporary sculpture by the French Lalane brothers:*

RIGHT AND TOP RIGHT *Outdoor sitting areas are positioned at each end of the balcony, which wraps around the house.*

ABOVE *Elisabetta's earliest artwork hangs between the toy shelves in her son Alexander's room. She painted this scene from the book* Les Fables de La Fontaine *when she was eight years old.*

OPPOSITE *In one of the guest bedrooms an old oak Italian bed inherited from Elisabetta's family commands attention. Despite its European provenance it looks perfectly at ease in its Asian setting. A majestic canopy is suspended from the ceiling.*

ABOVE *Laotion textiles by the American Carol Cassidy hang on a robe rack. Cassidy, who lives in Vientiane, is responsible for the rediscovery of the intricate textile tradition of Laos and her work is exhibited in museums worldwide.*

LEFT *The Chinese robe hanging above an Italian carved oak chest is a family heirloom brought to England by Peter's naval ancestors.*

EASTERN DECORATIVE ARTS

东方装饰的艺术

BELOW *A sinuous 17th-century table and chair made from fine-grained Huanghuali hardwood demonstrates to perfection the Chinese art of carpentry using mortise and tenon joints.*

OPPOSITE *Forming the centrepiece of an altar table is a Tang Dynasty pottery figure. Dating from around the 7th century, it dramatically depicts a tiger attacking a hunter on horseback.*

MORE THAN ANY OTHER decorative art, Chinese hardwood furniture embodies the restrained beauty and self-confident elegance of the East. Underlying the gleaming timber forms is a complex system of concealed mortise and tenon joints, developed by Chinese carpenters to allow for the region's climatic extremes, which put great strain on wooden constructions. The resulting pieces are a satisfying blend of harmonious lines and intricate detail. Their designs, many derived from earlier bamboo structures, and the warmth of the polished *huali* wood exude an almost universal appeal.

BELOW RIGHT *One of the essential calligraphy tools found on the desk of every Chinese scholar, highly polished hardwood brush pots from the late 17th or early 18th centuries.*

OPPOSITE *A dominant feature of Chinese interiors from the Ming Dynasty onward, and later popular in European homes, are lacquered screens painted or inlaid with floral motifs and auspicious symbols in jade and ivory. The jade disks are symbols of scholarly sophistication, while the stylized emblems of fruit and other plants signify prosperity and health.*

RIGHT *An intricate bamboo altar table dating from the 18th century features detailed supporting latticework. Such tables were used for religious offerings, or for displaying painted scrolls and calligraphy.*

BELOW *Remarkably modern in appearance, this Huanghuali tapered cabinet was crafted in the 17th century, its only decoration a set of lantern-shaped metal door pulls.*

RIGHT *Merchant boats were a popular motif in Chinese painting and porcelain. Here they are the subject of a table inlaid with a large porcelain panel in underglaze blue.*

BELOW *A distinctive feature of the mid-Qing Dynasty (1644–1911) was elaborately ornamented furniture. Characteristic of the era is this chair crowned with confronting dragons amid whirling clouds.*

LEFT The calligrapher's brush creates an evocative summer scene with simple yet fluid strokes. The artist's red seal in the bottom right-hand corner of the work is its mark of authenticity.

RIGHT This statuesque pottery horse from the Eastern Han Dynasty (A.D. 25–220AD) is like many that were buried in the tombs of princes and high-ranking officials.

ABOVE The restrained beauty of Chinese style is evident in these ornaments of carved coral, jade, agate, and enameled metal, incorporating archaic Chinese or later Buddhist motifs.

LEFT A horseshoe-shaped armchair from the 18th century is wrought here in bamboo, a popular alternative to the more sophisticated and expensive rosewood.

OPPOSITE Unlike that of its Asian neighbours, the furniture of China was elevated from early on. Here a grand, thronelike chair boasts a wide base of polished hardwood with dainty upturned feet, a wicker seat, and a back of deer antlers.

196

TOP RIGHT *A bed fit for an Empress, this ornate four-poster lacquered in deep red and gold dates from the 18th century. Fitted with a filmy white canopy, the bed is paired with a set of lacquered chests adorned with the traditional Chinese symbols of happiness and longevity.*

BOTTOM RIGHT *A deity from the pantheon of Buddhist gods, the stone figure of Tara, goddess of mercy, is a 10th-century antiquity from Indonesia.*

OPPOSITE *The modern face of Chinese art is represented by this massive outdoor sculpture in bronze by artist Ju Ming. Entitled* Taichi Thrust, *the 10-foot figure is one of several the sculptor has based on tai chi positions.*

ABOVE *Rich earthy colors and graphic motifs mark this pair of Ningxia pillar rugs from the early 19th century.*

RIGHT *Constructed without nails or glue in the characteristic Chinese manner, this Huanghuali six-poster canopy bed from the 18th century could be transported in parts and easily reassembled.*

199

HONG KONG LIFESTYLE
香港式生活

HONG KONG, THE ARCHETYPAL 24-hour city. A thriving metropolis, this city is home to over five and a half million people, 80 percent of whom live on less than 8 percent of the land. The pace of life is frenetic, and there is little escape from the swarming crowds and crawling traffic in the neon jungle of tower blocks, or from the ubiquitous sound of the jackhammer. Universally regarded as a paragon of capitalist virtues, Hong Kong society is all about hard work and competition. When they are not making money, people like to be seen spending it. We take a look here at some of the island's most fashionable haunts.

Let's start with what Hong Kongers do best: shop. The city is a favorite market of the world's top designer brands: Sales at Christian Dior, for example, doubled from 1995 to 1996; Hermès' two largest stores in Asia are both in Hong Kong.

Wealthy trendsetters with an eye for what's fresh from the catwalk go religiously to Joyce, Hong Kong's leading lifestyle store and the brainchild of style guru Joyce Ma. Her HK $50 million flagship outlet is as cutting edge in design as the range of fashions and homewares that it sells.

OPPOSITE *Perched above an alley in the heart of the Lan Kwai Fong district with its bars, nightclubs and restaurants, Le Jardin is a popular drinking spot on humid Hong Kong evenings.*

LEFT *Atmospheric Wanchai, once Hong Kong's notorious red-light district, is a maze of bustling shops, restaurants, street markets, and nightclubs.*

The buzzword among shoppers in Hong Kong and abroad is Shanghai Tang, the Chinese emporium with a whiff of the decadent style of 1930s Shanghai. Cheongsams and chopsticks, and Mao memorabilia such as velvet peak caps and watches, are given a modern twist, making People's Republic nostalgia today's fashion statement.

For traditional Chinese souvenirs, bargain cashmeres and silks, and the fakes that Hong Kong is famous for, Stanley Market on the south side of the island is everybody's fun day out. Temple Street

201

LEFT *Shanghai Tang is a must on the shopping circuit. David Tang's fashion emporium features Chinese silk shirts, dresses, and pajama suits in contemporary colors and cuts.*

RIGHT *The Hong Kong tradition of custom-made clothing is embodied in A-Man Hing, the city's oldest tailor and one of its best.*

Market, for much of the same, comes alive at night. Real Chinese products—embroideries, woks, and do-it-yourself acupuncture kits—often cost less than in mainland China at the city's Chinese government stores: China Products and China Arts and Crafts.

Surveys reveal you can get a better suit in Hong Kong than in Savile Row, and A-Man Hing Cheong, the oldest tailor here, tops the list for English style at a third of London prices. The details of regular customers—including bankers, lawyers, and Hong Kong's leaders—are written in old-style record books, and suits are still made on hand-operated Singer sewing machines.

Eating is as popular as shopping in Hong Kong and not often done at home. Streetside noodle stalls offer cheap, delicious fare, but are slowly losing out to upmarket restaurants, which open here by the week. The elite of the expatriate community pay top prices for Italian cuisine at Va Bene, while aspiring young brokers sink beers at Le Jardin. Both are in Lan Kwai Fong on Hong Kong island.

The talk of Island East, Hong Kong's new business district, is Q, a restaurant where the ultra-

ABOVE *Patrons of the popular La Dolce Vita bar in Lan Kwai Fong spill out onto the sidewalk. Bars like this take their inspiration from Hong Kong's many tiny noodle shops and street stalls.*

OPPOSITE *The Chinnery Bar at the Mandarin Oriental Hotel oozes traditional British style. Founded as a gentlemen's club, it only recently began admitting women.*

modern design is as alluring as the food. Executives opt for a Mediterranean lunch while working on their laptops. At Causeway Bay, Hong Kong island's shopping Mecca, the hot spot for Cali-Asian cuisine is Oscars, with its fresh, light food and sleek, contemporary decor.

Hotel restaurants, with international chefs serving some of the best food in town, are always fully booked with tourists and locals alike. A current place to be seen is Felix, the Philippe Starck-designed top-floor restaurant of the Peninsula, with panoramic views over the harbor. Go to Petrus at the Island Shangri-La for the best French food in town, to Yu at the Regent for the best fish, and to the Mandarin Grill at the Mandarin Oriental (the favorite rendezvous of the local business community) for the finest traditional fare in salubrious surroundings whether for breakfast, lunch, or dinner.

Afternoon tea is a regular engagement among Hong Kong's tai tais, the monied ladies who lunch. They nibble at scones and petit fours at the Clipper Lounge in the Mandarin Oriental, or the Tiffin Lounge in the Grand Hyatt, Hong Kong's most

ABOVE A favorite haunt of well-heeled expatriates, the exclusive Va Bene restaurant marries a rustic Italian ambience with fine dining.

LEFT The Cohiba Cigar Divan at the Mandarin Oriental Hotel on Hong Kong island is named after Cuba's most famous export, offering an extensive range of Havana cigars.

OPPOSITE *The distinctive hand of French designer Philippe Starck has created a futuristic look for the Felix nightclub at the Peninsula Hotel in Kowloon. Swirling glass obelisks glowing in Martian green and ruby red serve as bar tables.*

RIGHT *In an unusual play on conventional room planning, the minimalist Felix men's room enjoys million-dollar views over Kowloon harbor.*

BELOW RIGHT *Smart new nightclubs open every month in Lan Kwai Fong, but Club 97 remains the heart of hip nightclubbing in Hong Kong.*

lavish hotel. Health-conscious style victims go to Joyce Café, which swaps cake plates for Hong Kong's best martinis at 5 P.M. Afternoon tea often follows a beauty appointment at the city's most prestigious salon, Le Salon Orient Beauty, which offers the latest international treatments in a palatial environment.

Meanwhile, Chinese tycoons indulge in smoking fat cigars at the Tabacalera Cigar Divan in the Island Shangri-La, and the Cohiba Cigar Divan in the Mandarin Oriental, with its unparalleled range of Havana cigars.

The most nostalgic of Chinese restaurants is the Luk Yu Tea House, where waiters serve baskets of dim sum from trays slung around their necks, and bills are still calculated on an abacus. Fook Lam Moon has long been one of the most prestigious and expensive Chinese restaurants. Hong Kong continues to pulsate long into the night at JJ's, California's, and Club 97, the oldest and still the hippest club in town. The neon boulevards of Wanchai provide a more colorful form of nighttime entertainment.

Just as Hong Kong's contours recall the Manhattan skyline, like New York the island could certainly claim to be "the city that doesn't sleep." 完

BELOW *The Cohiba Cigar Divan at the Mandarin Oriental Hotel offers a club atmosphere for enjoying the world's finest cigars. The smoking lounge is decorated with patterned Spanish tiles and the warm wood tones of mahogany, echoing the interior style of Cuba. Strategic lighting creates the illusion of floating smoke rings.*

BOTTOM *Among the sandy shores and rocky coastline of Hong Kong's south side nestles Repulse Bay, a golden strip of beach backed by dense forested mountains. One of its highlights is The Verandah, a graceful colonial-style restaurant. Once part of the grand Repulse Bay Hotel, The Verandah retains its old-world atmosphere, providing an elegant escape from the tropical sun and tourist beaches.*

ABOVE *The mountains of Hong Kong's south side provide a dramatic backdrop for the beautifully manicured fairway of the members-only Shek O 18-hole golf course. Secluded at nearby Shek O beach are some of the island's most luxurious homes.*

OPPOSITE *When not eating out, Hong Kongers with the space to do so love nothing better than to entertain at home. This Italianate mansion with extensive formal gardens perches high above the famous Happy Valley racecourse, and was designed to create a flowing space for entertaining, with the dining room opening out onto a courtyard and pool.*

VISITOR'S GUIDE

访客指引

SHOPPING

RONALD ABRAM JEWELLERS
Mandarin Oriental Hotel
5 Connaught Road, Central
Tel. 2810 7677

BOOKAZINE LTD
Room 102/03
Alexandra House, Chater Road, Central
Tel. 2521 1649

ASCOT CHANG SHIRT MAKERS
MW6 Peninsula Hotel,
Kowloon
Tel. 2366 2398

A-MAN HING CHEONG TAILORS
Mandarin Oriental Hotel,
5 Connaught Road, Central
Tel. 2522 3336

LANE CRAWFORD
Levels 1-3, The Mall,
1 Pacific Place
Tel. 2454 3564

CHRISTIAN DIOR
Ground Floor, St George's Building,
2 Ice House Street, Central
Tel. 2526 0912

HERMÈS
Ground Floor,
08-09 The Galleria, Central
Tel. 2525 5900

JOYCE
The Galleria,
9 Queen's Road, Central

MARGUERITE LEE
The Galleria,
9 Queen's Road, Central

KAI YIN LO JEWELRY
Shop 373, Pacific Place,
88 Queensway, Admiralty
Tel. 2524 8238

PETRUS AND LA TABACALERA
Island Shangri-La, Pacific Place,
Supreme Court Road, Central
Tel. 2877 3838

LE SALON ORIENT BEAUTY
13 Duddell Street,
Central
Tel. 2524 7153

SEIBU
Unit 110, Pacific Place,
Admiralty

SHANGHAI TANG
Ground Floor, Pedder Building,
12 Pedder Street, Central
Tel. 2525 7333

STANLEY MARKET
Temple Street, Tsimshatsui

SHOPPING CENTERS

THE LANDMARK
Des Voeux Road, Central

PACIFIC PLACE
Queensway, Admiralty

PRINCE'S BUILDING
Chater Road, Central

SWIRE HOUSE
Connaught Road, Central

ARTS & ANTIQUES

ALTFIELD GALLERY
248.9 Prince's Building
10 Chater Road, Central
Tel. 2537 6370

BANYAN TREE
Prince's Building,
10 Chater Road, Central
Tel 2523 5561

GRACE WU BRUCE
701 Universal Trade Center,
3 Arbuthnot Road, Central
Tel. 2537 1288

CHINA ARTS & CRAFTS
Star House, Salisbury Road,
Tsimshatsui

HANART T Z GALLERY
The Old Bank Of China Building,
Bank Street, Central
Tel. 2526 9019

CHARLOTTE HORSTMANN &
GERALD GODFREY LTD.
Ocean Terminal Kowloon
Tel. 2735 7167

SANDRA WALTERS
28 Arbuthnot Road,
Central
Tel. 2522 1137

RESTAURANTS & CLUBS

BENTLEY'S
The Basement,
Prince's Building, Central
Tel. 2868 0881

CALIFORNIA'S
California Tower,
Lan Kwai Fong, Central
Tel. 2521 1345

THE CHINA CLUB
12th Floor,
The Old Bank of China Building
Bank Street, Central
Tel. 2840 0233

CLUB 97
9 Lan Kwai Fong, Central
Tel. 2810 9333

COO SEIBU
The Mall, Pacific Place
88 Queensway, Admiralty
Tel. 2971 3333

FELIX
Peninsula Hotel,
Salisbury Road, Kowloon
Tel. 2366 6251

FOOK LAM MOON
35 Johnston Road, Wanchai
Tel. 2866 0663

GADDI'S
Peninsula Hotel,
Salisbury Road, Kowloon
Tel. 2366 6251

GODOWN
Hotel Furama Kempinski,
1 Connaught Road, Central
Tel. 2524 2088

GRISSINI'S
Grand Hyatt Hotel,
1 Harbour Road, Wanchai
Tel. 2588 1234

LE JARDIN
10 Wing Wah Lane,
Lan Kwai Fong, Central
Tel. 2526 2717

JJ'S NIGHTCLUB
Grand Hyatt Hotel,
1 Harbour Road, Wanchai
Tel. 2588 1234

JOE BANANAS
23 Luard Road, Wanchai
Tel. 2529 1811

JOYCE CAFE
Exchange Square, Central
Tel. 2810 0807

LUK YU TEA HOUSE
24 Stanley Street, Central
Tel. 2523 1970

MANDARIN GRILL &
CAPTAIN'S BAR
Mandarin Oriental Hotel,
5 Connaught Road, Central
Tel. 2522 0111

MICHELLE'S
2 Lower Albert Road,
Central
Tel. 2877 4000

OSCARS
Podium 3, World Trade Centre,
280 Gloucester Road, Causeway Bay
Tel. 2861 1511

PEAK CAFE
121 Peak Road, The Peak
Tel. 2849 7868

Q
33 Tong Chong Street, Quarry Bay
Tel. 2960 0994

STANLEY'S FRENCH
Stanley Main Street, Stanley
Tel. 2813 8873

STANLEY'S ORIENTAL
90b Stanley Main Street, Stanley
Tel. 2813 9988

TALK OF THE TOWN
34th Floor,
281 Gloucester Road,
Causeway Bay
Tel. 2837 6786

THE VERANDAH
109 Repulse Bay Road,
Repulse Bay
Tel. 2803 1001

TOKIO JOE
16 Lan Kwai Fong, Central
Tel. 2525 1889

VA BENE
58-62 D'Aguilar Street,
Lan Kwai Fong, Central
Tel. 2845 5577

WYNDHAM STREET THAI
38 Wyndham Street,
Central
Tel. 2869 6216

YU
Regent Hotel,
Salisbury Road, Tsimshatsui
Tel. 2721 1211

HOTELS

CONRAD
Pacific Place,
88 Queensway, Admiralty
Tel. 2521 3838

HOTEL FURAMA KEMPINSKI
1 Connaught Road, Central
Tel. 2525 5111

THE GRAND HYATT
1 Harbour Road, Hong Kong
Tel. 2861 1234

ISLAND SHANGRI-LA
Pacific Place,
88 Quensway,
Admiralty
Tel. 2877 3838

THE MANDARIN ORIENTAL
5 Connaught Road, Central
Tel. 2522 0111

MARRIOTT
Pacific Place,
88 Queensway, Admiralty
Tel. 2810 8366

THE PENINSULA
Salisbury Road,
Kowloon
Tel. 2366 6251

THE REGENT
18 Salisbury Road,
Kowloon
Tel. 2721 1211

RITZ CARLTON
3 Connaught Road, Central
Tel. 2877 6666

SHANGRI-LA KOWLOON
64 Mody Road, Tsimshatsui
Tel. 2721 1111

MUSEUMS

THE HONG KONG MUSEUM OF ART
Salisbury Road,
Tsimshatsui

THE HONG KONG MUSEUM OF HISTORY
58 Haiphong Road,
Kowloon Park, Kowloon

MIDDLE KINGDOM
Ocean Park, Hong Kong
Tel. 2552 0291

MUSEUM OF CHINESE HISTORICAL RELICS
Causeway Center,
28 Harbour Road, Wanchai

MUSEUM OF TEA WARE
Flagstaff House,
Hong Kong Park

SAM TUNG UK MUSEUM
Kwu Uk Lane,
Tsuen Wan, New Territories

SUNG DYNASTY VILLAGE
Kowloon
Tel. 2741 5111

LEISURE ACTIVITIES

THE HONG KONG GOLF CLUB
Fanling, New Territories
(Three 18-hole Courses)
Tel. 2670 1211
Deepwater Bay
(One 9-hole Course)
Tel. 2812 7070

HONG KONG JOCKEY CLUB
Happy Valley
Tel. 1817 Enquiries

ROYAL HONG KONG YACHT CLUB
Kellett Island,
Causeway Bay
Tel. 2832 2817

SIMPSON MARINE
Chinese Junk Hire
Tel. 2555 8377

VICTORIA PARK
Tennis & Squash
Causeway Bay
Tel. 2570 6186

INDEX

Albert, Prince, of Monaco 55
Allen, Nick 169
    table *168*
architect: apartment *46-51*, 47-8
Armitage, Kenneth: sculpture *82*
Arrighi, Lucianna: drawings *82*
Art Deco *49*, 153, *154, 155*
    house *166*, 167-9, *168-75*

Bancel (sculptor): bird *72*
Bank of China *27*
bars *200, 202, 203*
Beatles: photographs 20, *22*
beds:
    Ching Dynasty *72*
    daybed *14*
    four-poster *199*
    Italian *188*
    Ming *15*
    opium *39*
    six-poster canopy *199*
    sleigh *111*
Biedermeyer furniture *48, 49*
Bloomfield (artist) painting *184*
bonsai garden *124-9, 125-6*
bookcases: Biedermeier *48*
Boyd, Arthur: painting *121*
Brazier-Jones, Mark 169
    furniture *134, 167, 171, 173*
    torchère *168*
Bruce, Grace Wu 13, 15
Buddhas:
    Burmese *187*
    Siamese *34*, 35
Buddhist knots of destiny *93*
Bunyarak, Harry:
    apartment *160*, 161-2, *162-5*
    paintings *165*

cabinets:
    medieval-style *167*
    Ming *16*
    moon-lock *164*
    17th-century Chinese *195*
Caine, Michael 55, 63
calligraphy 15, *16*, 70, *196*
calligraphy tools *192*
Campenelli : canvases *146*

carpets:
    local *28*
    Ningxia pillar rugs *199*
    "runway" 97, *98*
Cassidy, Carol: textiles *189*
ceramics see pottery, porcelain
and ceramics
chairs:
    bamboo *196*
    Ching Dynasty *122, 163*
    Egyptian throne *134*
    glass *149*
    Italian *166*
    klismos *122*
    Louis XVI *44, 140*
    metal wing *171*
    Ming *13, 17*
    Ming-style *160, 165*
    Qing Dynasty *195*
    rattan *41*
    17th-century Chinese *192*
    thronelike *197*
    chaises longues:
    18th-century *184*
    le Corbusier *50*
Chan, Kamwa and Michelle 19-20
chandeliers:
    Bohemian crystal 76, *76*
    crystal *79*
    Czech *47*
    French fire-gilded *108*
    Indian *31*
    Taiwanese *181*
Chater, Sir Paul 29
Chau, Kai Bong and Brenda:
    house *176-81*, 177-9
Chau, Sir Sik-Nin 180
Chemiakin (artist) 82
paintings *84*
Chen Jialing: paintings *85*
chests:
    Italian *189*
    lacquered *199*
    Ming *17*
Chi Park Lai 25
China Club *152-9*, 153-4, 157
Chinese family: house *130-7*,
131-2

Ching Dynasty:
    bed *72*
    chairs *122, 163*
    porcelain *162*
    table *95*
Chiu Ya Tsai: paintings *16, 158*
chopsticks: silver-plated *161*
Chow, Wailee: renovated house
    146-51, 147-9
clubs *204*, 211-12
China Club *152-9*, 153-4, 157
colonial houses:
    jungle hideaway *182-9*, 183-5
    Macanese *102-11*, 103-4
    terrace *68-73*, 69-70
commode: Italian *44*
Convention Plaza *141*
Costner, Kevin 61
Crawley, Nigel: paintings *171,
175*
Cunningham, Scott 169
    furniture *169, 170, 171*

Dao Hai Phong: paintings *162,
164*
d'Auriol, Yan and Sandra: house
    68-73, 69-70
Davies, David 35
desk: Ming-style *165*
Diana, Princess of Wales *31*
dragon: Chinese sculpture *124*
Dufour, Nicole: paintings *72, 73*
Dufy, Raoul: painting 149

Edward VIII 31
Elizabeth II *33*

feng shui 25, 26, 64, 132, 173
Fortuny: lamp *22*
Foster, Norman 27
Friend, Donald: paintings 120
furniture:
    Biedermeier *48, 49*
    Chinese 192
    French *23*
    Italian *44*
    lacquer *44*
    Liaigre *23*

Ming 13-15, *13-17*
modernist 47, *50, 51*
shagreen *148*

garden: private *124-9, 125-6*
glassware:
    Czech 74, *90, 91*
    etched *158*
    Murano *90, 91*
gold: house of *176-81*, 177-9
golf course *208*
Government House *24-6, 25-6,
28-33,* 29

Gray, Eileen 47, 48
Guanyin (goddess): sculpture *128*

Hai Tien: paintings *80, 84*
Hamisky (sculptor): wrought-iron
    sculpture *72*
Han Dynasty: figures *86, 196*
Happy Valley:
    house *209*
    private garden *124-9, 125-6*
    small apartment *160*, 161-2,
    162-5
Harilela, Dr Hari 75-6
Harilela family: home *74-9*, 75-6
Henderson, Gerard: painting *37*
Henry, Alison 55
    apartment *34-9*, 35-6
Hon Chi Fun: painting *80*
Hong Kong and Shanghai Bank
    27
hotels 35, 139, 205-7, *205, 206,
208*, 212
Howard, Cecil: paintings *72*
humidor *39*
Hunter, Peter: interior designs
    94, *95-7, 96-9*
Hurel, Philippe: soft furnishings *96*

Iglu (lifestyle shop) *18*, 19, *23*
Irons, Jeremy 55
Isogai, Rensuke 29

Jackson, Simon:
    apartment *118-23*, 119-20

triplex designed by *138-45,*
139-42
jade 76, 179, *194*
Jardine Matheson:
Shek O house *112-17,* 113-15
trade paintings 185
Jebson, Jacob 107
Jebson & Co. 103
Ju Ming: sculpture *81, 198*
junk: home on *52-7,* 53-5

Kang Dynasty: table *92*
Kangxi period: blue-and-white
porcelain *163*
Khmer:
artifacts 162
sculpture *73*
Kirchher, Astrid: photographs *22*

lacquerware: Japanese *91*
Lalane brothers: sculpture *186*
Lan Kwai Fong *200,* 202, 207
Lane, Danny 169
furniture *149*
Lauren, Ralph: linens *54*
Le Corbusier 47
furniture *49, 50*
leisure activities 212
Liaigre, Christian: furniture *23*
lifestyle 201-2, 205-7
lifestyle shop *18, 19, 23*
lighting:
crystal lamps *138*
multilevel lamps *138*
quartz and rock lanterns *134*
Lin Fengmian: painting *12*
Lin Sanzhi: calligraphy *16*
Lindemann, Ina 104
Linley, David: humidor *39*
Liu Shau Kwan 82
Liu Wei: painting *64*
Lo, Kai-Yin 87-8
Long March: ceramic figures
depicting *157*

Mackintosh, Charles Rennie:
furniture *51*
malachite: Russian *76*
Mallinson, Elisabetta and Peter:
jungle hideaway *182-9,* 183-5
Marcos, Imelda: dinner service
118
markets 201-2
Memphis Group pedestal *48*
Michael, Desiree 104
Michael, Hans: colonial-style
house *102-11,* 103-4

Ming Dynasty 87
furniture 13-15, *13-17, 98*
Ming style:
chairs *160, 165*
desk *165*
minimalism 97
mirrors:
contemporary *169*
18th-century *173*
English *64*
Gothic-Revival *66*
Thai *38*
Mount, Sally and Duncan: house
166, 167-9, *168-75*
Moy, Willy: photographs *147*
murals:
Egyptian design *175*
stained-glass *177, 181*
museums 212

nightclubs *206,* 207, 211-12

opium pipes *35*
ornaments *196*

pagoda: gold *180*
Palace Style: table *92*
parrots: ceramic 115, *116*
Patten, Chris 25, 29, 31
Patten, Lavender 25, 29
The Peak: house on *34-9,* 35-6
pearls: portrait in *180*
Pei, I.M. 27
pianos *67, 148*
Portuguese colonial-style house
102-11, 103-4
pottery, porcelain and ceramics
43
animals *124, 126-7*
blue-and-white *40, 162, 163*
Ching *162*
Han Dynasty figure *196*
Japanese *91*
Long March figures *157*
parrots 115, *116*
Sung Dynasty 87
Tang Dynasty figures *116, 193*
teapots *42*

Qing Dynasty: chair *195*

Regency: chair *122*
Renoir, Pierre Auguste: painting
55, *56*
Repulse Bay 29, 208
restaurants 202, 205-7, *205, 208,*
211-12

Rietveld, Gerrit 47
furniture *50*
Rousseau, Garrison: furniture
148
rugs see carpets

Sai Kung: house in *60-7,* 61-3
Scarampi del Cairo di Pruney,
Elisabetta and Galeazzo:
apartment *40-5,* 41-3
screens:
Japanese-style *116*
lacquered *194*
sculpture:
antiquities *92*
Cambodian *169*
ceramic animals *124, 126-7*
Chinese *124*
French *186*
Khmer *73*
outdoor *198*
Taiwanese *81*
Tang Dynasty *70*
semainier: imitation Boulle *120*
Shanghai Museum of Art 13
Shaw, Sir Run Run 169
Shek O 208
house in *112-17,* 113-15
shopping 201-2, *202,* 210-11
silverware 35
ashtray *153*
Cambodian *19, 35,* 43
Chinese *34*
chopsticks *161*
Thai *163*
Tibetan 161-2, *163*
Sipek, Boris: chandelier *47*
sofa: Louis XV *173*
Sotsass, Ettore: table *19*
Starck, Philippe:
furniture *48, 206*
lamp *20*
stone figures: Indonesian *199*
Streisand, Barbra: dining chairs
118
Sung Dynasty: pottery *87*

Tabar, Kambiz 53-5
tables:
altar *193, 195*
Art Deco *49*
bar *206*
British *135*
Chinese *51*
Ching Dynasty *95*
coffee *173*
console *169*

convertible to chair *48*
glass *160*
Italian *19, 166*
ivory-inlaid *90, 91*
Kang folding *92*
marble *166*
Ming *16, 98*
Palace Style *92*
porcelain-inlaid *195*
17th-century Chinese *192*
Tai Ping: carpet *28*
Tang, David:
China Club *152-9,* 153-4, 157
house *60-7,* 61-3
shops 63, 202
Tang, Richard: garden *124-9,*
125-6
Tang, Sir S. K. 126
Tang Dynasty: figures *70,* 116,
193
Tao Ho 25
teapots *42*
terra-cotta figures *69, 86*
Terry, Marie 113, 115
textiles: Laotian *189*
tiles, floor: Macao *71*
Ting, Walasse: painting *84*
torchères *134, 168*

Villa d'Oro *176-81,* 177-9
visitor's guide 210-13

Walker, William 169
Wallem Shipping Company 113
wallpapers: French *111*
Walters, Richard 81
Walters, Sandra: apartment *80,*
81-2, *82-5*
Wanchai 20, *20,* 201, 207
Wang Shixiang 14
Wong, Harold: painting 14
Wu Guanzhong: paintings *16,* 88,
88, 89

York, Duchess of 63
Young, Sir Mark 26

Zhang Daqian 16
Zhu Xin Jian: painting *83*
Zuber: wallpaper *111*

Acknowledgments

Photographs

Additional photographs were contributed by:

Pascal Blancon 30, 31, 52, 68, 200, 202tr, 208tl bl

Keith Macgregor 4, 58, 100, 144, 190, 201

courtesy of Grace Wu Bruce Co. Ltd. 13, 192l, 195br tr, 196, bl, 199br

courtesy of Altfield Gallery 163

courtesy of Post 97 205tl

courtesy of Hanart Gallery 198

courtesy of Sandra Walters 196 tl

courtesy of Shanghai Tang 161, 202tl

courtesy of La Dolce Vita 202br

Interior photographs were taken using Kodak film courtesy of Kodak Film Hong Kong

The publishers have attempted to contact the copyright owners of literary works from which extracts have been taken in this book. The publisher apologises if inadvertently permission has not been obtained from a copyright owner to include any extract from a copyright work.

With thanks

The publishers would like to extend special thanks to Benjamin Creutzfelt at Christie's for his contribution to the chapter on Eastern Decorative Arts, and to Simon Jackson for all his help. Many thanks also to Garrison Rousseau, Altfield Gallery, Grace Wu Bruce, Sandra Walters, Hanart Gallery, Alison Henry Design, Hazel Wong, David Tang, Lynn Henchman, Karen Howes of The Interior Archive, Libby Willis, Peggy Vance, Mandarin Oriental Hotels for their support, and all those in Hong Kong who graciously allowed their homes to be photographed.